Ivatt & Riddles Locomotives

Haresnape

Ivatt & Riddles Locomotives

A Pictorial History by Brian Haresnape

IAN ALLAN LTD

First published 1977

ISBN 0 7110 0795 0

© Brian Haresnape 1977

Published by Ian Allan Ltd, Shepperton, Surrey,
and printed in the United Kingdom by
Ian Allan Printing Ltd

Contents

Foreword by David Shepherd   *7*
Introduction   *8*

R. A. Riddles. The 'Austerities'   *18*
     Section 1   2-8-0 Ministry of Supply (WD) General Duties   *18*
     Section 2   2-10-0 Ministry of Supply (WD) General Duties   *28*

H. G. Ivatt. The Final Years of The LMS   *34*
     Section 3   2-6-0 Class 2F Mixed-Traffic   *34*
     Section 4   2-6-2T Class 2P Mixed-Traffic   *40*
     Section 5   2-6-0 Class 4 Mixed-Traffic   *46*

R. A. Riddles. The BR Standard Locomotives   *52*
     Section 6   4-6-2 Class 7 Mixed-Traffic ('Britannias')   *53*
     Section 7   4-6-2 Class 6 Mixed-Traffic ('Clans')   *62*
     Section 8   4-6-0 Class 5 Mixed-Traffic   *66*
     Section 9   4-6-0 Class 4 Mixed-Traffic   *70*
     Section 10   2-6-4T Class 4 Mixed-Traffic   *74*
     Section 11   2-6-0 Class 4 Mixed-Traffic   *78*
     Section 12   2-6-0 Class 2 Mixed-Traffic   *82*
     Section 13   2-6-2T Class 3 Mixed-Traffic   *84*
     Section 14   2-6-2T Class 2 Mixed-Traffic   *88*
     Section 15   4-6-2 Class 8P Express Passenger   *90*
     Section 16   2-6-0 Class 3 Mixed-Traffic   *94*
     Section 17   2-10-0 Class 9F Heavy Goods   *98*

Appendix 1   The LMS Diesels   *107*
Appendix 2   Named Locomotives   *109*
Bibliography   *112*

Left: WD 2-8-0 No 90044, standing at York shed on 23 October 1965./*E. F. Bentley*

Title page: Close-up of Caprotti Class 5 4-6-0 No 73150, showing arrangement of valve gear, and twin mechanical lubricators driven off rear coupled wheel. The later type of cab is clearly seen; this had a fallplate between tender and cab. No 73150 (with 5MT power classification above number) was photographed at St Rollox shed on 17 May 1964./*P. H. Groom*

Below: Of the various locomotive classes described in the pages that follow, no less than 32 engines of Riddles design and 11 of Ivatt design have been preserved, or earmarked for preservation. David Shepherd's 2-10-0 No 92203 *Black Prince* is one of the engines permitted to run in steam over BR tracks from time to time, and is seen here at Longmoor, soon after purchase for preservation./*A. Swain*

Foreword

'What do you want to buy those things for?' The question came from a railway enthusiast who, it seemed, not only questioned how other people should spend their own money, but who was so entrenched in the pre-nationalisation era that he considered any locomotive built after 1948 as 'modern rubbish'.

It was 1967, and I had just purchased my very own Standard Class 4MT and Standard 9F — on the telephone, to British Railways! At this time our great steam age was dying, fast. There was not much choice remaining in these last days of steam, but in retrospect £5,800 does not seem bad value for 75029 and 92203, bearing in mind that both engines were in mint condition, and both were purchased straight out of service, with spares.

I care not if the ancestry of a particular class of locomotive can be traced to Swindon or Doncaster, Crewe or Brighton. It is the aesthetic appeal of all steam engines that attracts me, through the eyes of an artist. I do, however, happen to think that a double blast pipe 9F is one of the most impressive of all locomotive designs.

As the steam age passes into history there is surely no longer room for the insular and parochial attitude of my intolerant friend. The Standards and 'Austerities' are now being deservedly recognised as fine machines. Some were better than others. Their functional design, with the accent on ease of maintenance, took precedence over any aesthetic appeal they might have had, and this upset many died-in-the-wool purists. Nevertheless I believe that in the final reckoning such designs as the standard 9F, undoubtedly the most successful, will prove worthy of all the locomotives that preceded them.

To those of us who most particularly recall the last years of steam on Britain's railways, this pictorial survey of Ivatt and Riddles locomotives will give hours of pleasure. The many fine photographs will evoke nostalgic memories of those last 25 years, whether they portray shining 'Britannias' in full cry or work-weary 2-6-2 tank engines going about their humble duties.

The tragedy of these locomotives has been their short working lives — I have already owned No 92203 *Black Prince* for longer than British Railways!

David Shepherd

Introduction

For the first 30 or so years of their railway careers the rise to seniority of the two men whose locomotive designs form the subject of this book led them along remarkably similar paths. Both H. G. Ivatt and R. A. Riddles had started as apprentices at Crewe Works on the London and North Western Railway, Ivatt in 1904 and Riddles in 1909. By the time they were called upon to serve their country in the Great War, Ivatt was Assistant Outdoor Machinery Superintendent at Crewe and Riddles was a fitter at Rugby. Both found themselves out of a job when the war ended, and Ivatt took the post of Deputy Locomotive and Carriage and Wagon Superintendent at Stoke Works on the North Staffordshire Railway; Riddles was able to return to Rugby, but in 1920 he was appointed Assistant to the Works Manager at Crewe.

The Railway Amalgamation of 1 January 1923, with Hughes appointed as CME for the new LMSR, resulted in the run-down and closure of the Stoke Works. In these early years of the LMS, Riddles was still at Crewe. Soon there were further changes, and with Stoke closed and Hughes replaced by Sir Henry Fowler as CME, Midland influence became dominant in LMS locomotive affairs and Ivatt was appointed Special Assistant to Fowler at Derby. In 1928 he became Works Superindendent at Derby, and Riddles was his assistant. Together, they set about the problems of locomotive repair work so effectively that they reduced the number of engines under repair at any given time from an average of about 150 to 60. The second batch of Fowler's 'Royal Scot' class 4-6-0s was constructed at Derby under their supervision.

In 1931 Riddles was again at Crewe, this time as Assistant Works Superintendent, and he was in this post when W. A. Stanier was appointed as CME*, and the first Pacific, No 6200 *The Princess Royal* was built at Crewe whilst Riddles was there. Stanier then

* This period of locomotive design, on the LMS, is the subject of a companion book in this series, entitled Stanier Locomotives, *a pictorial history, by the same author.*

Below: Wakefield motive power depot, with WD 'Austerity' 2-8-0s awaiting their next turn of duty. In the foreground are Nos 90370 and 90381, both sporting the usual coating of grime, which seemed to emphasise their austere and basic appearance; photographed at the time when these sturdy engines were still an integral part of the Yorkshire railway scene./*Eric Treacy*

Top right: The powerful Stanier two-cylinder 2-8-0 design of 1935 for the LMS, was initially chosen by the Ministry of Supply for quantity production to meet the urgent needs of World War II transportation. New batches were ordered and some existing engines were requisitioned, and given WD numbers. The class saw service in various parts of the Middle East, and some went to Italy. The Riddles Ministry of Supply 2-8-0 'Austerity' design was based upon the Stanier 2-8-0, but every detail was scrutinised for ease of manufacture and economy in materials, so their final appearance was very different indeed. One of the WD Stanier locomotives is seen here, as WD No 70579, which started life as LMS No 8020 then became WD No 579, then Iran No 41-151; photographed at Port Said on 3 March 1948, whilst awaiting return to Britain./*Peter W. Gray*

appointed Riddles as his Principal Assistant, at Euston, whilst Ivatt became Mechanical Engineer, Scotland, at St Rollox. In October 1937, the two men exchanged jobs, with Riddles taking over at St Rollox as Electrical and Mechanical Engineer, Scotland.

The Stanier era on the LMS was an exciting and stimulating time for all involved, as that great railway at last received the powerful and efficient standard locomotives it so badly needed. By 1937 there were sufficient new engines to have made a real impact upon the day-to-day running, and the emergence of the first streamlined Pacific, No 6220 *Coronation*, was a highlight of British steam locomotive

Left: Engines of war preserved. Riddles MOS 'Austerity' 2-8-0, No 1931 of the Swedish State Railways, with chimney extension and electric headlights, alongside Stanier 2-8-0 No 8431, built by the GWR at Swindon in 1944. Both are preserved on the Keighley and Worth Valley line./*G. W. Morrison*

Below: Probably the last surviving Riddles 'Austerities' to operate in steam, excepting preserved engines, were the 2-10-0s taken over by the Greek and Syrian railway systems (see page 28), which were believed to still have them, or some of them, in stock at the time of writing, although the Greek engines were no longer regularly steamed. The Greek engines were their Class LB Nos 951-966, and were used on both passenger and goods work. No 958 was photographed at Xanthis, with the fireman busy getting the coal forward on the eight-wheel tender. The cab roof has an added heat shield and a small awning projects over the side window — both measures taken to keep the cab interior reasonably cool. The four Syrian engines were reported to be working passenger trains between Aleppo and Cobanbey in August 1975./*David Dixon*

development. Riddles was on the footplate of this magnificent engine when a new world rail speed record for steam was set up, approaching Crewe at 114 mph. Plans already existed for further development of the streamlined train; later these were for a larger 4-6-4 design, with mechanical stoker. All in all it seemed as though LMS locomotive affairs were on the crest of a wave.

However, even as plans were laid to take a complete LMS 'Coronation Scot' train across to America for exhibition purposes, the ominous signs of war in Europe were gathering strength, and the spring of 1939 found the two men engaged in strikingly different missions. H. G. Ivatt, at the time Principal Assistant to Stanier at Euston, was engaged upon war preparation work, including a War Office requirement for a new tank — of the fighting variety, not the locomotive! — of which some 5000 were ultimately built, including 200 at Crewe works. R. A. Riddles, on the other hand, was proudly exhibiting the LMS train to an eager American public. The 1939 'Coronation Scot' was a luxurious affair, with air-conditioned rolling stock which would have set new standards for high-speed British rail travel. The engine No 6220 *Coronation* (actually No 6229 *Duchess of Hamilton*, renumbered) and the train, were painted in a striking livery of crimson lake with gold stripes. The big Pacific was probably the finest of Stanier's productions, and after a tour of 38 American cities and towns during which it

covered 3120 miles of US railroad tracks, the complete train was exhibited at the New York World's Fair, which opened on 30 April that year, and some two million people had inspected the train by the time the exhibition ended.

The outbreak of World War II left the 'Coronation Scot' stranded in the United States. Riddles had been delegated to bring the train back once the World Fair was over, but he was asked to take charge of and form a new Directorate of Transportation Equipment, for the Ministry of Supply. Not until 1940 were arrangements made for the return of No 6229 (alias 6220) to Britain, whilst the splendid new carriages remained in the States throughout the war, and were used as a club for Army Officers.

Thus, two of Stanier's Principal Assistants became embroiled in the urgent war effort and the peacetime era of speed and streamlining was halted, in full steam. Stanier himself was later appointed as a Scientific Advisor to the Ministry of Production, and C. E. Fairburn became Acting CME. For a while the locomotive affairs of the LMS had to take a back seat.

Even before war was declared the Ministry of Transport had announced that the War Office would require locomotives for use overseas. This was an urgent requirement when Riddles took up the Directorate, and the new 2-8-0 and 2-10-0 designs he produced form the subject of the first part of this book.

Left: American Class S160 2-8-0 design produced to the order of the Ministry of Supply and built to the British loading gauge. Designed by Major J. W. Marsh of the US Army Corps of Engineers and built by the three major locomotive firms, Baldwin, Alco and Lima. The first engines were scratch-built, without full production drawings! No 1879 is seen whilst on loan to the LNER in 1943/4; fitted with vacuum brake equipment, it had two cylinders 19in diameter by 26in stroke; coupled wheels 4ft 9in diameter; boiler pressure 225lb psi; and total weight of engine and tender in full working order was 124 tons 5 cwt. Engines of the class were still in steam in Eastern Europe, at the time of writing./*Author's collection*

Below: Another view of one of the American-built 2-8-0 'Austerity' locomotives, a design ordered by the Ministry of Supply in World War II, some of which ran on Britain's railways before use on the Continent and elsewhere towards the end of the war. The experience gained with these engines, which had items such as rocking grates and self-cleaning smokeboxes, undoubtedly influenced H. G. Ivatt when considering labour-saving devices for his post-war LMS designs. Of the 390 engines delivered to Britain, only one remained in steam in post-war days; this was WD No 93257, which ran on the Longmoor Military Railway. The engine is seen here working the 7.10am Liss-Longmoor train near Liss Forest on 9 July 1951; it was named *Major General Carl R. Gray Jnr./P. M. Alexander*

Bottom: The Ministry of Supply selected the standard six-coupled saddle tank of the Hunslet Engine Company for production in modified form as an 'Austerity' shunting engine for use during World War II. Riddles was responsible for the modifications but the overall design cannot, of course, be credited to him. As in the case of his WD 2-8-0 and 2-10-0 engines, the emphasis was upon cheap and rapid construction, with expensive steel castings and forgings replaced by welding and fabrication. A total of 377 engines was delivered between 1942-5 and after the cessation of hostilities many found their way to industrial lines, including the NCB. Illustrated is an example owned by the Port of London Authority; seen as their No 85./*Collection: A. Swain*

Above: The LNER purchased 75 war-surplus 'Austerity' 0-6-0ST and classified them J94; most of them were based in the North-East. Three of the class, Nos 68008/15/43, are seen here on works shunting duties at Darlington in February 1960. Construction of these popular engines for industrial use continued until 1964, by which time no less than 484 had been built. A number survive in Army ownership, or in the ownership of preservation groups./*P. F. Winding*

Riddles was also responsible for the modification of an existing 0-6-0ST for war use. The design of his tender engines was deliberately austere and simple, and they were constructed more than twice as fast as was possible with the Stanier engines.

So urgent was the need for locomotives that orders were also placed with American locomotive builders for a similar 2-8-0, the first of which was built without proper production drawings, which were then made from it! These USA class S160 engines were shipped to Britain to await the invasion, many being put to work in this country. Their labour-saving devices impressed H. G. Ivatt, who subsequently introduced such features to the LMS, and produced in his Class 4 2-6-0 a very American-looking machine, complete with high running-plate.

The 0-6-0ST already referred to was an adaptation of the existing Hunslet standard shunter for industrial railway systems. Riddles made some changes to the materials used in its manufacture for cheapness and speed of

construction, with complete success, and no less than 377 were built by six locomotive builders, who speeded up production considerably. After the war the design was still produced for many years as an industrial shunter, and many examples remain in steam at the time of writing.

The 2-10-0 version of the 'Austerity' was a truly remarkable machine and deserves a place high on the honours list of classic British steam locomotive design. It arose from a need for an engine with a lower axle load than the 2-8-0, capable of working long and heavy supply trains over light or improvised tracks. The engine had a larger boiler, with a wide firebox and rocking grate, and seemed capable of steaming on even the poorest of fuel. Of 20 engines which were sent to the Middle East, some examples remain today in Greece and Syria — what finer tribute could there be to a design never intended to have a lengthy lifespan, but produced solely for the urgent needs of war!

In August 1943 Riddles returned to the LMS, and took the post of Chief Stores Superintendent. H. G. Ivatt, remained as Principal Assistant to Stanier, and then to Fairburn, who was appointed first Acting CME, and then CME, when Stanier resigned from the LMS in 1944. For his services in the Ministry of Supply, R. A. Riddles was awarded the CBE in the 1943 New Year Honours List. Whilst Riddles had been away, the LMS workshops had been intensively engaged on war work, including the manufacture of aircraft parts and armaments, as well as coping with locomotive and rolling stock

Above: C. E. Fairburn's development of the Stanier 2-6-4T. Prior to the introduction of the BR standard Class 4 2-6-4T design, a batch of these engines was built at Brighton works for use on the Southern Region, numbered 42066-42106. An LMS 1945 Derby-built locomotive, No 42210, is seen here piloting Stanier 'Black Five' No 45109 on a down parcels train, climbing past Grayrigg./*Ivo Peters*

repairs and maintenance, and new construction. By 1944 it was possible for the drawing office to re-awaken its ideas on locomotive development and to consider the needs of the railway once peace was restored to the nation. H. G. Ivatt took an increasingly important part in steam locomotive design from about this time, because Fairburn was primarily an electrical engineer and was also suffering from declining health. The only new steam locomotive design produced, which can be credited to Fairburn, was the modernised version of Stanier's two cylinder 2-6-4T. Fairburn died suddenly in October 1945 and Ivatt succeeded him as CME in January 1946. Riddles was a little taken aback by this, as he thought that the job might well go to him, but very shortly afterwards he was appointed to the higher position of Vice-President of the LMS — the man to whom Ivatt then became responsible!

Stanier had introduced the taper boiler conversion of the 'Royal Scot' class, but after initial application of the boiler to two 'Jubilee' 4-6-0s, it was left to Ivatt to carry on the rebuilding of the 'Royal Scot' engines and to make similar modifications to a number of the Fowler 'Patriot' class.

Ivatt brought proper attention to bear upon the problems of locomotive servicing and maintenance. New designs would have to take these features into full account. The desperate labour problems of wartime had emphasised the deficiencies of existing locomotive design in this respect, and Ivatt was impressed — as already mentioned — by the American 2-8-0s, with their self-cleaning smokebox,

rocking firegrate and hopper ashpan with bottom doors. He adapted these features to LMS conditions and incorporated them in his own new designs, and in new construction of Stanier's engines. Two final Stanier Pacifics were built, with modifications by Ivatt, and he produced a whole series of experimental versions of the classic Stanier 'Black Fives' with improved bearings, alternative valve gears and some with double blast pipes and chimneys.

The three new designs produced by H. G. Ivatt in the final years of the LMS form the content of the second part of this book. Even during the war years some thought had been given to the design of new lightweight goods and passenger engines, to replace the pre-Grouping types still used on secondary services. All manner of proposals (some obviously done more as 'flights of fancy' than in earnest) had been put forward by the Derby drawing office, including bizarre 0-6-0s with bar frames, wide fireboxes, and stovepipe chimneys, but Ivatt was able to determine the

13

Above: Ivatt continued the programme of re-boilering the Fowler 4-6-0s which Stanier had initiated with the 'Royal Scot' class. The smaller 'Patriot' 4-6-0s were to be rebuilt with the superb Crewe 2A boiler and given improved cab, tender and modified cylinders. Only 18 engines were actually converted, and uprated from 5XP to 6P, out of the class total of 52. In experimental apple green livery, with LNWR-style lining, No 45531 *Sir Frederick Harrison* was photographed at Birmingham New Street on 21 June 1948./*T. J. Edgington*

true need and to produce his thoroughly up-to-date and efficient 2-6-0 and 2-6-2T designs. So successful were these modest new types that further construction was authorised by the Railway Executive for use on other Regions in the early years of nationalisation, and they were adopted, with only minor changes, as BR standard classes. Ivatt must also be credited with the introduction of main-line diesel traction to this country, and his prototypes form the subject of an Appendix, on page 107.

From the streamline dream of 1938 to the post-war reality of a state railway system was just ten short years. When Britain's Big Four railway companies were merged into one national system, in 1948, they were in poor shape. The ravages of war had taken a toll on maintenance and staff, and the painstaking climb back to pre-war standards of maintenance and operation was clearly going to be a long one. Despite Ivatt's diesels and the similar locomotives produced by Bulleid for the Southern (not forgetting the venture into gas turbine traction by the GWR) it seemed certain at that time that steam traction still had a long future on Britain's railways, with perhaps electrification as the eventual replacement. But the future type of steam locomotive could no longer be the aerodynamically-shrouded multi-cylinder

piece of sophistication of the late 1930s. As Ivatt had shown on the LMS, new designs had to be extremely functional and the emphasis had to be upon ease of servicing and operation. Staff shortage and an increasing reluctance for new recruits to work in the filthy conditions existing in some areas meant an emphasis upon labour-saving devices and ease of access to all working parts.

The new world of nationalisation was peopled by committees, and the very powerful position of CME at the head of the various committees involved in traction affairs went to Riddles, who was appointed Member of the Railway Executive for Mechanical and Electrical Engineering. With him went a team, composed largely of ex-LMS men, who took a leading role in co-ordinating the work that took place on the design of new standard locomotives, carriages and wagons. R. C. Bond and E. Pugson were the Chief Officers for Locomotive and for Carriage and Wagon Construction and Maintenance respectively. E. S. Cox was the Officer responsible for Design, for all types of rolling stock. G. S. Hussey dealt with administration and C. M. Cock (from the Southern) was the Chief Officer, Electrical Engineering. To begin with, the four CMEs of the main line railway companies remained in their respective offices. H. G. Ivatt was the last to go, in 1951, and with him the title of Chief Mechanical Engineer lapsed.

The whole story of the testing of existing locomotive types (including the 1948 Locomotive Exchange Trials) and the subsequent development, design and construction of the new BR standard steam locomotives, has been thoroughly and admirably chronicled by E. S. Cox, one of the men intimately involved. The very readable books he has written are listed in the Bibliography on page 112, and are thoroughly

Above: Two superb Pacifics which incorporated a number of new features were introduced by H. G. Ivatt in 1947/8. Basically of Stanier design, the two engines had Timken roller bearings on all axles, except the bogie, on engine and tender; rocking grate; self-emptying ashpan and self-cleaning smokebox. The trailing truck was re-designed and the rear end of the frames, the reverser and the cab side sheets were modified compared to Stanier's 'Coronation' Pacifics. When new, the engines were both fitted with electric lighting. No 46256 *Sir William A. Stanier FRS* was photographed in BR crimson lake livery, after removal of electric lighting, and fitting of AWS, about to leave Stafford station on an up express./*J. B. Bucknall*

Left: The classic Stanier 'Black Five' mixed-traffic two cylinder 4-6-0 was developed by Ivatt for further construction up to 1951. There were a number of deviations from the standard design, and one of the Caprotti valve gear engines No 44755, which also has a double chimney, electric lighting and Timken roller bearings, is seen here. In plain black livery, with interim BR lettering on the tender, the locomotive was photographed working the 1.55 pm Leeds-Edinburgh train in the heart of the Yorkshire Pennines, in the shadow of Pen-y-Ghent. Ivatt's modifications did not enhance the appearance of the Stanier design! One locomotive, No 4767, was fitted with outside Stephenson valve gear. It was done in order to investigate the effect of variable versus fixed lead on otherwise identical engines; no advantage was found./*Eric Treacy*

Bottom left: The final Ivatt version of Stanier's 'Black Five', with the running-plate raised high, in American-fashion, to expose the driving wheels and valve gear. No 44687 was photographed at Patricroft shed, with BR lined black livery. The engine had SKF roller bearings, Caprotti valve gear and double chimney. The location of the top feed, on the first ring of the taper boiler, was a feature of Ivatt's engines, and the top feed was of improved design. These two engines, Nos 44686/7 were not delivered until 1951, by which time the first BR standard Class 5 4-6-0s were in service./*J. R. Carter*.

15

recommended to all who seek deeper knowledge of this final phase of British steam locomotive design. The present work is intended as a companion, not a repetitive study, and as such I have carefully avoided using the same illustrations, whilst Mr Cox has co-operated by checking the manuscript for accuracy in reportage.

The BR standard locomotives form the subject of the last part of this book. In ascribing their overall design to R. A. Riddles, it must be emphasised that they were the product of team work, with the various drawing offices having an important role to play. There was nothing *new* about these engines (except perhaps the cab layout); they were the intelligent amalgam of the best of existing practices, as viewed against the economic and other factors affecting the

railways at that time. Function dictated form and accessibility, and simplicity dictated layout, and yet they were attractive in a modest way and all had a strong family likeness. As David Shepherd has observed in his Foreword to this book, they had tragically short lives, which was in no way a reflection upon their design or service performance. In discussion with Mr Riddles, when I was finalising the contents of this book, he observed that locomotive design was an art rather than a science. If one looks at his final creation for British steam, the 9F 2-10-0, I suggest that Riddles produced a masterpiece!

Biographical accounts of both H. G. Ivatt and R. A. Riddles have been published in recent years* and both are recommended for further information on the lives of these two men, who together shaped the final phase of steam design in Britain perhaps more effectively than any of their contemporaries. If their names are not associated with the more glamorous phases of the British steam locomotive saga it is because of circumstances beyond their control, but perhaps there is a different sort of glamour, or romance, in contemplating the tremendous

*Master Builders of Steam *(including H. G. Ivatt) by H. A. V. Bulleid (Ian Allan Ltd) and* The Last Steam Locomotive Engineer: R. A. Riddles CBE, *by Colonel H. C. B. Rogers, OBE. (George Allen & Unwin).*

Below: Two stages in design proposals for an up-to-date replacement for the numerous 0-6-0 goods engines on the LMS, as described in the text. The lower illustration (b) was conceived along 'Austerity' lines and would have had a singularly unattractive appearance, with stovepipe chimney and no running plate, plus 'Austerity' type cab and tender. The earlier proposal (a) was more in the Stanier tradition. Ivatt insisted upon a 2-6-0 wheel arrangement, to improve riding, and the final solution was his Class 4F, introduced in 1947 and subsequently developed as the BR standard Class 4 Mogul.

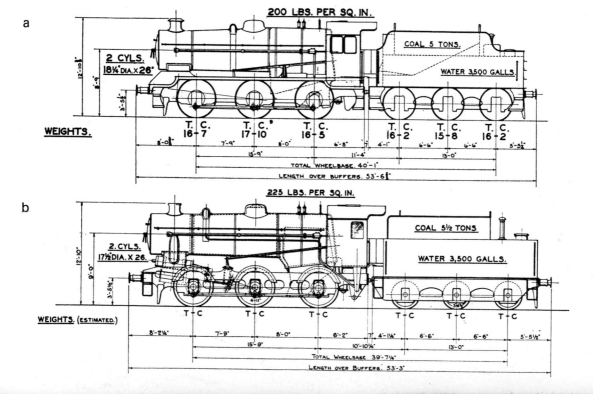

contribution made by Riddles during World War II. When we met to discuss this book he showed me a letter he had received in February 1945 from Major-General D. J. McMullen, Director of Transportation, who had just visited the British Liberation Army, fighting in Holland. McMullen wrote: 'Everyone loves the 2-10-0. It is quite the best freight engine ever turned out in Great Britain and does well on even Belgian "duff", which is more like porridge than coal. The 2-8-0s have trouble for steaming on this muck alone, but if they can get 25 per cent Dutch lump coal mixed with it they do all right'. McMullen then went on to observe that he had travelled on a Riddles 2-8-0 only three miles behind the German front line and had seen the shell bursts in the battle area, from the footplate, at Nijmegen station. 'So your products are well up into the fighting area, often ahead of the medium artillery positions', he added.

Without the generous assistance of three men, the job of compiling this pictorial survey would have been onerous indeed and I wish to place on record my sincere thanks for all their kindness. Firstly to R. A. Riddles, for patiently explaining the role he played in the design of the engines ascribed to him, and for vividly retelling the story of his days on the LMS into the bargain; to E. S.Cox, for going out of his way twice on my account to collect and return the manuscript and illustrations and for checking the text (not to mention making

some subtle suggestions for altering shades of meaning in my original draft!) and to Peter Rowledge (whose knowledge of locomotive history never ceases to amaze me), in particular for providing the background story to the overseas wanderings of the 'Austerities' without which the book would have been incomplete.

In my search for specific illustrations I have had the invaluable help of the following people, and to them (and all the photographers whose work appears on these pages) I am extremely grateful: H. C. Casserley; G. H. Daventry; G. W. Morrison; S. C. Nash; Jonathan Smith and Alec Swain. I would also like to thank A. B. MacLeod and the Ian Allan Library for much assistance in the early stages of the compilation of the book.

Brian Haresnape FRSA NDD
Box Hill, Surrey
May 1976

Below: H. G. Ivatt's austere and functional post-war Mogul, developed as a modern replacement for the numerous inside-cylinder 0-6-0 goods engines, many dating back to pre-Grouping days. The raised running plate and labour-saving devices were in line with American practice, as seen on the Class S160 USA Transportation Corps 2-8-0s which had run in Britain during World War II. No 43050 was the first of a batch built for use on the Eastern/North Eastern Regions in 1950, at Doncaster./*British Rail ER*

R. A. Riddles

The 'Austerities'

In September 1939, on the day war broke out between Britain and Germany, R. A. Riddles was appointed Director of Transportation Equipment; this was a new part of the Ministry of Supply. His responsibilities were wide and covered all types of equipment including railways, docks and harbours, inland water transport, and the War Department fleet. Large numbers of locomotives were urgently needed to aid the war effort, but Riddles and his team also supplied cranes, bridges (including the famous Bailey Bridge,) jerricans and Mulberry harbour piers and pontoons. Riddles returned to the LMS in August 1943, by which time design work had been completed on his 2-8-0 and 2-10-0 engines, of which no fewer than 1085 were built for the War Department.

Below: WD 2-8-0 No 7074, built by Vulcan Foundry in 1943, showing the layout of the Westinghouse air brake compressor. The steel and cast iron driving wheel centres were made from similar patterns. Balance weights were cast integrally with the centres and no allowance was made for the reciprocating parts. Special wartime oil lamps on front bufferbeam.
/Ian Allan Library

2-8-0
Wartime General Duties Locomotives
Introduced: 1943
Total: 935*
BR Power Class: 8F
Ministry of Supply (Austerity) WD

The adoption of a standard type of locomotive for military use was a practice well proven by experience in World War I, when the Robinson Great Central Railway 2-8-0 heavy goods engine had been selected for war service overseas. The same engines were again considered, by Riddles in 1939, when locomotives were required for shipment to France to support the British Expeditionary Force. The Robinson design, however, was rejected, largely because over the years the numerous engines of the class had been modified by their operators to a degree where they could no longer be considered as constituting one standard class. A further problem was their width over the outside cylinders. This was too great to allow them to run on a number of important British lines, and meant that, once peacetime had returned, it would be difficult to dispose of any new engines of the type that had been built for war needs.

*Grand total of locomotives constructed; of these 733 were subsequently taken into BR stock.

The immediate needs of the BEF in France were met by requisitioning more than 100 of the GWR Dean goods engines of the 2301 class 0-6-0 design, soon after the outbreak of war. Many of the engines were on the Continent at the time of Dunkirk, and some of them were engines which had seen similar service in the 1914-18 war. They were, however, too small for the haulage of the heavy ammunition and supply trains, which it was envisaged would be required in the forthcoming battle for survival. Riddles was faced with an urgent demand for new engines of greater power, to be delivered as quickly as possible. Having rejected the Robinson design, he was sure that the most suitable existing locomotive was the excellent Stanier LMS 2-8-0. A total of 240 was ordered for the War Department, of which 208 were actually built, and some existing LMS engines were also transferred to WD stock. The intention to ship these engines to France was thwarted by the

Below: Ministry of Supply 'Austerity' Class 2-8-0.

Bottom: WD 'Austerity' 2-8-0 No 7195 was delivered in September 1943 with armour plating over the top of the boiler and the cab. It ran in this bizarre form on the Melbourne and Longmoor Military Railways, but the armour (which added some three tons deadweight to the engine) was removed before the engine was shipped to the Continent.
/Collection: R. A. Riddles

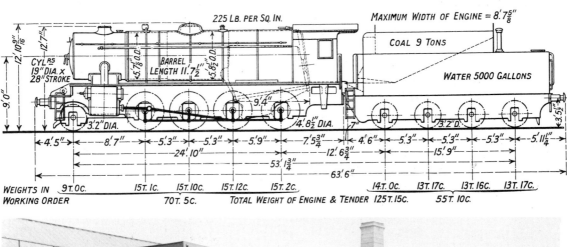

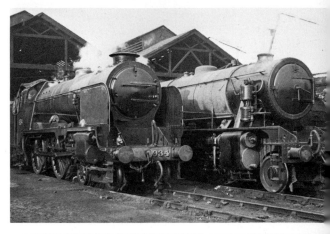

Top right: Bricklayers Arms shed, with Riddles MOS 'Austerity' 2-8-0 No 7422, in WD livery, alongside 'Schools' class 4-4-0 No 934 *St Lawrence.* The 2-8-0 was one of the first to arrive for work on the Southern Railway, which eventually had 50 engines allocated in 1943-4. The LMS had 50 and the LNER had 350. The GWR subsequently received 89 2-8-0s (to replace American engines); these were transferred from the other railways to the GWR. All were later sent abroad, as the war reached its final phase in Europe and there was a desperate need for motive power to restore working to the Continental rail network. No 7422 was renumbered 77422 when all WD numbers were increased by 70000 in September 1944, to avoid duplication with existing locomotive numbers in Britain and elsewhere. Note the tarpaulin blackout covers over the cab and tender of the 'Schools' Class 4-4-0./*S. C. Townroe*

Centre right: The scene: Dover. The time: early 1945. By then the WD locomotives had become an integral part of the final fight for freedom, as World War II drew to a close. The D-day landings found much of the Continental railway system in damaged or destroyed state, and their locomotives run-down or inoperable. The shipment of WD engines, by train-ferry, to France was a vital part of the operation to restore the transportation system and to move troops and supplies. Twenty-two new 2-8-0s are seen here, as they await their cross-Channel voyage. Despatch to France commenced in 1944 and included the 450 engines which had been running in Britain in 1943/4./*Ian Allan Library*

Below: No less than 450 of the 'Austerity' 2-8-0s were on loan to Britain's main line railways in 1943/4. They were transferred to the WD in the winter of 1944/5 and after some storage they were gradually shipped to Europe, where they were used by the British Army in France, Belgium, Holland and Germany. Some were operated by the US Transportation Corps. No 77230 is seen on home metals, working a freight over the GW and GC Joint line, on Ruislip troughs. The WD livery varied from a khaki-green, or brown, to a richer 'army' green. In all, no less than 932 2-8-0s operated on the Continent; only Nos 77223, 77369 and 79250 were not sent./*C. R. L. Coles*

Nazi advance, and the withdrawal of the defeated Allied force to Dunkirk. Nevertheless, the Stanier engines were of immense value to the war effort both on the home railways (more were built, by the SR, GWR, and LNER for use on their lines) and in the Middle East, and later Italy. The Stanier design also saw service in Iran, Turkey, Persia, Egypt and The Western Desert. Some of the Robinson 2-8-0s were also sent to the Middle East, so urgent was the need for more locomotives in 1941.

It now became clear that when the planned invasion of France materialised, a very large number of new locomotives would be needed, to support the invasion forces. Both German sabotage and Allied bombing would take their toll of the existing locomotives on the Continent, and it would be necessary to have a large stock of suitable engines ready for shipment and immediate use. Orders were placed with American firms for a new utility 2-8-0 design, as discussed in the Introduction on page 12, and these would be used to support the US troops in Europe when the time came, with a number being put to work on Britain's railways in the meantime.

For the British-built contribution, Riddles could have continued with further orders for the Stanier 2-8-0s, but two factors made him consider the possibility of producing an entirely new engine. First there was the amount of man-hours required for the construction of the Stanier 8Fs, and second there was the problem of a serious shortage of much of the material used in them, in particular the steel castings and forgings. Some 22 tons of steel castings were used in each engine. If engines were to be built both quickly and cheaply, the Stanier design would not be the ideal. Accordingly, Riddles planned a new engine, with simplicity in manufacture, maintenance and operation in mind; avoiding sophisticated design features, and replacing expensive and difficult-to-obtain materials with more basic solutions. The choice of 'Austerity' as a descriptive name for the new design was indeed an apt one, and was chosen by Riddles at an early stage of the

Below: An 'Austerity' in Paris. The 2-8-0 was photographed leaving St Lazare, Paris with a British Army troop leave train, composed of 17 carriages of former LNWR, GWR and Midland Railway origin, taken over by the War Department. Note the covered third rails for the Paris Region Ouest suburban electrification, in the foreground./*L. Hermann*

Right: In December 1946 the LNER purchased 200 ex-WD 2-8-0s for their permanent locomotive stock, and classified them Class O7. These became Nos 3000-3199 and were purchased at a price of £4500 each, together with 24 spare boilers. In LNER livery, No 3085 was photographed at Stratford Works on 4 June 1947, awaiting attention to the left-hand cylinder and valve motion. When taken into BR stock Nos 3000-3100 became Nos 90000-90100 and Nos 3101-3199 became Nos 90422-90520. The locomotive illustrated here started life as WD No 78516, built in 1944, and served in Belgium, before returning to Britain. Many of the LNER engines retained the Westinghouse air brake, until taken into BR stock. /*H. C. Casserley*

Bottom right: Between November 1945 and June 1946, the bulk of the WD engines were returned to Britain, leaving 185 2-8-0s in Holland; three more were destroyed in collisions in Holland during 1945. There were also five on the Detmold Military Railway. After repairs most of the engines were put to work on the LNER, GWR and SR, with a total of 481 at work in Britain by July 1948; the remainder were placed in store, except for engines still used by the Army. WD 2-8-0 No 77467 was photographed passing Pelaw Junction, in December 1951. Air brake equipment has been removed from side of smokebox. /*C. C. B. Herbert*

planning, to impress upon all concerned exactly what his objectives were.

The North British Locomotive Company, in Glasgow, co-operated with Riddles over the design and manufacture of the new engine, which was to be a 2-8-0 along broadly similar lines to the Stanier design, but with a parallel boiler and round top firebox, in place of the expensive taper boiler and Belpaire firebox, and with only 2½tons of steel castings instead of 22tons, a reduction achieved by making

Above left: During 1946-7 the Crown Agents for the Colonies arranged for the purchase and overhaul of 12 WD 2-8-0s, for use on the Kowloon-Canton Railway. The overhauls took place at Woolwich Arsenal, and six engines were despatched from London Docks in October 1946, with the second six following a year later. The engines had electric headlights, buckeye couplings and a pilot below the bufferbeam. Ex-WD No 77269, was photographed as KCR No 27, standing in Kowloon Station, Hong Kong in April 1955./*G. H. Daventry*

Above: With the rich green paintwork positively gleaming, and the front of the smokebox finished in silver, former WD 2-8-0 No 77269, now No 27 of the Kowloon-Canton Railway, was photographed outside Kowloon Shed in April 1955. Air brake retained, and added ventilation provided for the cab, with sliding louvred shutters to side windows, a necessity in the hot and very humid climate which prevails in the area for at least eight months of the year./*G. H. Daventry*

extensive use of cast iron. Production of the engines was to be a rush job, with the engines coming straight off the drawing board. There was not time to produce a single prototype, or run extensive trials, before proceeding with quantity production. The first engine appeared on 16 January 1943 five months after the date of placing the order, and it was assembled in ten days once all the parts had been delivered; this was a record for the North British Locomotive Company.

The principal dimensions of the 'Austerity' 2-8-0 were as follows: two cylinders 19in diameter by 28in stroke; coupled wheels 4ft 8½in diameter; boiler pressure 225lb psi; tube heating surfaces 1512sq ft; firebox heating surface 168sq ft; superheater heating surface 310sq ft; grate area 28.6sq ft. Tractive effort at 85per cent boiler pressure was 34 215lb. Major differences from the Stanier 2-8-0 were an increase of ½in in the cylinder diameter, and the provision of an eight-wheel tender with 1000gal more water; the capacity was 5000gal of water and 9tons of coal.

The appearance of the 'Austerity' design was surprisingly neat and did not offend the eye, despite the complete lack of ornamentation and the very plain stumpy chimney (which was 3in lower than the other boiler mountings.) The economies in production were mainly achieved by the use of fabrication in place of steel castings and forgings, as already mentioned, and examples of this fabrication included the axlebox guides, brake hangers and spring link brackets, reversing rod and shaft. Cast iron was used for the cylinders, blast pipe, smokebox saddle (which had the exhaust passages formed in it), chimney and front-end cylinder covers. High-duty cast iron was used for the coupled wheel centres except for the third, main pair, which were steel castings; all the centres were made from similar patterns. The leading truck and the tender wheels were rolled in one piece. Originally, the tender wheels were of chilled cast iron, but following early troubles with this feature, rolled forged wheels were substituted. The boiler was of simple design and the clothing consisted of steel plates carried on

Top: The War Department retained two 'Austerity' 2-8-0s for use at Longmoor, where the Army trained engineers in railway operations. These were Nos 77337 and 79250, which were later renumbered WD (later AD) 400/1 respectively. Both were named, with No 77337 becoming *Sir Guy Williams* and No 79250 *Major General McMullen.* Working bunker-first on a Longmoor Military Railway passenger train, No 77337 is seen whilst converted to oil-firing. The engine still had the wartime numbering, but the buffer beam of the tender carried the later number WD400. This locomotive was badly damaged at Soham, Cambridgeshire on 2 June 1944 whilst hauling a munitions train which exploded, and received a new boiler when returned to Glasgow for repair./*Author's collection*

Above: In December 1948 the Railway Executive decided to purchase 533 'Austerity' 2-8-0s, at a price of £2,929 each, and these, together with the 200 ex LNER Class O7 engines, made up a total of 733, which became Nos 90000-90732 in the BR

stock-book. When purchased, the 533 engines were all taken into Eastern Region stock, irrespective of the Region to which they were allocated to for operating purposes. Of this total of engines purchased, 108 were in store at the time at various places on the Eastern and Western Regions. Swindon took the WR allocation in hand and made some modifications of their own, as seen here on No 90323, which has a new casing for the top feed and a housing on the right-hand running plate, ahead of the cab, for the fire irons./*Brian E. Morrison*

Right: Another "Westernised" 'Austerity' 2-8-0, No 90355, photographed at High Wycombe on 28 March 1959 with a down goods. The WR style of lampbrackets have been fitted, including additional brackets at the front end over the right-hand cylinder (for spare lamps), and the top feed has a proper casing. The air brake equipment was removed from the WD engines operated by British Railways./*W. G. Putnam*

crinolines with the necessary insulation against heat loss being provided by the air space between the plates and the boiler proper. Westinghouse and vacuum brakes were provided for train working, and the engine was steam braked. The all-welded tender had provision for a water scoop to be fitted, if needed at some future date.

The engines were built as follows:

Nos 7000-7049	North British	1943
Nos 7050-7059	Vulcan Foundry	1943
Nos 7060-7109	Vulcan Foundry	1943
Nos 7110-7149	Vulcan Foundry	1943
Nos 7450-7459	Vulcan Foundry	1943
Nos 7150-7449	North British	1943/4
Nos 7460-7509	Vulcan Foundry	1943/4
Nos 800- 879	North British	1944
Nos 8510-8624	North British	1944/5
Nos 8625-8671	Vulcan Foundry	1944
Nos 8672-8718	Vulcan Foundry	1944
Nos 9177-9219	Vulcan Foundry	1944
Nos 9220-9262	Vulcan Foundry	1944/5
Nos 9263-9312	Vulcan Foundry	1945

In September 1944 the WD numbers were increased by 70000 to avoid duplication with existing locomotives. Nos 78518 and 78560 were the first to be so numbered by North British, and No 78715 was the first to be delivered from Vulcan with the new numbering. Existing engines were soon altered.

Until October 1944 all the 2-8-0s were allocated for use in Britain as they were delivered from the builders, and no less than 450 were on loan to the main lines at this time. From October 1944 to November 1945 all these, together with new engines stored at various points, were shipped to Europe, for use by the British Army in France, Belgium and Holland, in the wake of the thrust towards Germany. Sometimes the Riddles engines were only a few miles behind the front lines, as the fight for freedom continued and vital supplies and ammunition were needed urgently.

The Netherlands Railways (Nederlandsche Spoorwegen) took over 227 of the 2-8-0s and gave them NS running Nos 4301-4527. In June 1946, an exchange took place, with 53 of these 2-8-0s being returned to Britain for a like number of the 2-10-0 version (see page 29.) The State Mines Railways in Holland also used the Austerity 2-8-0s between 1944-46 and had six in all, of which three were returned to the WD in 1946 and three went to the NS.

In 1946-47 twelve of the 2-8-0s were acquired by the Kowloon-Canton Railway (British Section,) these were as follows:

WD No 70805	KCR (BS) No 23
WD No 70820	KCR (BS) No 28
WD No 77268	KCR (BS) No 22
WD No 77269	KCR (BS) No 27
WD No 77450	KCR (BS) No 30
WD No 77478	KCR (BS) No 26

Above: With a long climb ahead, a Tyne Dock-Consett iron ore train is seen heading towards Annfield Plain, with WD 2-8-0 No 90074 providing banking assistance to Class O1 2-8-0 No 63755, on 14 August 1962. In the final years of steam BR standard 2-10-0s were used on these workings, as illustrated on page 102./*J. M. Rayner*

WD No 77490	KCR (BS) No 25
WD No 77509	KCR (BS) No 24
WD No 78659	KCR (BS) No 31
WD No 78660	KCR (BS) No 21
WD No 78694	KCR (BS) No 29
WD No 79237	KCR (BS) No 32

Nos 21-25 were converted to oil firing, whilst in 1954, No 25 was fitted with a new coal-fired boiler made locally. Some of the engines ran until 1963, with the first withdrawals taking place in 1957.

The final disposition of the class after their war duties were over may be summarised as follows:

LNER*	200
BR	533
Holland†	184
KCR	12
WD retained	2
Collision damage	3
Missing‡	1
Total	935

* *The LNER purchased 200 in 1946; their Class O7, (later absorbed into BR stock).*
† *Excludes 53 transferred away in June 1946 in exchange for 53 2-10-0s. 52 eventually went to BR.*
‡ *No 79189 cannot be accounted for after leaving the NS.*

The 'Austerities' were built at roughly twice the rate it had been possible to build the Stanier engines and Riddles' aims were fully realised, with a class total of 935. Only the LNWR Ramsbottom DX goods 0-6-0 bettered this total for a single class of British steam locomotive. As can be seen from the above list, 733 eventually returned to service on British Railways and it says much for their basic good design that they survived in quantity until the final phase of BR steam operations. They were much appreciated by shed staff for their ease of maintenance, whilst footplatemen found them free-running and strong. Ironically the large BR fleet all went to the scrapyards and when the preservationists cast their eyes around for examples, the only two survivors were in store in Sweden. Both have now returned to Britain for preservation albeit in somewhat altered state.

First of class withdrawn: 90083 (1959)**
Last of class withdrawn: 90682 (1967)**
Examples preserved: WD Nos 79257/9‡‡

** *These were the first and last in the BR stocklist. In Holland withdrawals commenced in 1949 and ended in 1958, with the exception of two locomotives purchased by the Swedish State Railways (SJ). The Kowloon-Canton Railway examples were withdrawn between 1957-63, the last one being No 29 (ex WD 78694).*
‡‡ *The preserved engines are former SJ Nos 1931 and 1930 respectively.*

Below: 'Austerity' repatriated. WD No 79257 was sent to the Netherlands in 1945, and became NS No 4464. In about 1951 it was sold, with one other, to Swedish State Railways (SJ). In Sweden it was altered from the original design by the provision of an all-enclosed cab (for use north of the Arctic Circle) by having the tender wheelbase shortened to six wheels, and by the fitting of standard SJ boiler fittings and steam heating equipment. It became SJ No 1931 and from 1958 it was stored against strategic emergency, in full working order. In January 1973 it was returned to Britain, for use on the Keighley & Worth Valley Railway. The engine was photographed on 21 April 1974, working a train out of Keighley. The cab had to be modified to fit the KWVR gauge and the tall chimney (see picture on page 9) was removed; small snowploughs were retained below the buffer beam./*G. W. Morrison.*

SECTION 2

2-10-0
Wartime General Duties Locomotives
Introduced: 1943
Total: 150*
BR Power Class: 9F
Ministry of Supply (Austerity) WD

The 'Austerity' concept was further developed by providing an engine of basically the same tractive power, but with the maximum axle load of the preceding 2-8-0 reduced from the already moderate figure of 15¾tons, to the very low value of 13½tons. This was done in order to provide an engine which might be used on very lightly laid, or even improvised tracks. Such an engine had to be able to negotiate sharp curves in spite of the length of wheelbase, and Riddles produced a 2-10-0 design, with a bigger boiler and with a wide firebox. The centre coupled wheels were flangeless and those on each side had flanges of reduced thickness, which enabled the big engine to run through a 4½chain curve without derailment.

The most noticeable difference between the 2-10-0 and the 2-8-0, on which it was closely based, lay in the provision of the larger boiler

* Grand total of locomotives constructed; of these 25 were taken into BR stock

and wide firebox, and the use of a rocking grate similar to that used on the USA 2-8-0s (see page 10). The cylinder dimensions and coupled wheel diameter were the same as for the eight-coupled engines, and the tender was identical. The steel firebox was equipped with three arch tubes and was arranged for easy conversion to oil-firing.

Below: Ministry of Supply 'Austerity' Class 2-10-0

Right: 'Austerity' 2-10-0 No 73777 trundling along 'light engine' and bunker-first on a British main line. Prior to the construction of the 150 engines of this class only two examples of the ten-coupled steam locomotive had hitherto run on Britain's railways — the Decapod 0-10-0T of the Great Eastern and the 0-10-0 Lickey Banking engine of the Midland Railway. On the WD 2-10-0s the middle pair of driving wheels was flangeless, which together with the sideplay allowance and slightly flexible frames, enabled curves of 4½chains to be negotiated safely. The first 2-10-0 was No 3650 (later 73650), which was delivered from the North British Locomotive Co works early in December 1943 and ran trials on the LNER line between Glasgow, Craigendoran and Edinburgh. All the engines built up to November 1944 were put to work on Britain's railways. Twelve went to the LNER, the rest to the LMS; later the LNER engines also went to the LMS, which had 79 in total. These were all recalled between August and November 1944 for service overseas. The same year 20 engines were despatched to the Middle East Forces, WD Nos 73652-73660, 76372, 73682-73688; of these 16 went to Egypt and four to Syria. In 1945 a second batch was delivered, Nos 73750-73799. Of these, 30 went direct to the War Department and 20 to the LNER. Six of the War Department allocation were sent to the Longmoor Military Railway and the other 24 to the Continent./*E. R. Wethersett*

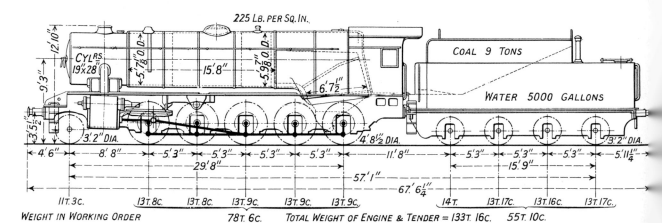

225 LB. PER SQ. IN.

12'10"

CYL^RS 19"x28"

5'7⅝" O.D.

15'8"

5'9⅞" O.D.

6'7½"

COAL 9 TONS

WATER 5000 GALLONS

9'3"

3'5½"

3'2" DIA.

4'8½" DIA.

3'2" DIA.

4'6" 8'8" 5'3" 5'3" 5'3" 5'3" 11'8" 5'3" 5'3" 5'3" 5'11¼"

29'8"

15'9"

57'1"

67'6¼"

11T. 3C. 13T. 8C. 13T. 8C. 13T. 9C. 13T. 9C. 13T. 9C. 14T. 13T. 17C. 13T. 16C. 13T. 17C.

WEIGHT IN WORKING ORDER   78T. 6C.   *TOTAL WEIGHT OF ENGINE & TENDER = 133T. 16C.*   55T. 10C.

Left: WD 2-10-0 No 73755 was the 1000th WD locomotive built in Britain and ferried to Europe since D-Day, and was named *Longmoor*. The engine is seen, attached to the 1001st, being loaded on to the train-ferry at Dover on 9 May 1945. The 2-10-0s were all shipped to the Continent with the exception of Nos 73651, 73774-73799 and the 20 already in the Middle East. In 1945 Belgium had 43 of the class and Holland had 60. Later in 1946 there were 103 in Holland when 53 more were sent there in exchange for the same mumber of 2-8-0s, which latter were returned to the UK. The NS (Nederlandsche Spoorwegen) gave the class numbers from 5001-5103 in their stocklist. Prior to this final allocation of 103 engines, 2-10-0s from both Holland and Belgium (50 all told) had operated in Germany on the Deutche Reichsbahn (British zone) to alleviate a shortage of power, in 1946./*Ian Allan Library*

Above: The Railway Executive purchased 25 of the 'Austerity' 2-10-0s in December 1948 and numbered them 90750-90774. Since the end of 1946, the 20 engines which the LNER had received direct from the makers in 1945 had been in store, and these, together with two from the LMS (which had received them from the Cairnryan Military Railway in March 1947) and three from Longmoor, which had never been steamed since their completion, formed the total. The last two engines built, Nos 73798/9 both carried the name *North British* for some odd reason, and still had these nameplates when they became BR Nos 90773/4. The latter was photographed at Eastfield, Glasgow on 21 June 1949, in ex-works condition. */H. C. Casserley*

Centre right: WD 2-10-0 No 90772, on road tests with the ex LMS Mobile Testing Unit, Dynamometer Car No 3, and a luggage van at Dumfries in June 1952. The locomotive was attached to the special corridor tender constructed by the LMS just prior to the outbreak of World War II, and it is interesting to note that the tender was still in fully lined crimson lake livery at this late date. The locomotive was in the standard BR plain black goods engine livery, with silver paint embellishments to the front end./*P. Webb*

Bottom right: Of the 20 locomotives sent to the Middle East in 1944, 16 went to Egypt and 4 to Syria. The Egyptian allocation later passed to the stock of the Greek railways becoming their Nos LB 951-966. The four Syrian engines were WD Nos 73685-73688, and when the Syrian railways were nationalised in 1946 they were renumbered 685-688. One of the 2-10-0s in Greece is seen here, No LB 956, photographed at Agros Ioannis depot, Piraeus, on 25 January 1964. The Greek 2-10-0s were converted to right-hand drive, with the air brake compressor moved to the left-hand side of the smokebox. Large electric headlight; deflector behind chimney and tropical-type cab roof added./*David Dixon*

Above: 'Austerity' 2-10-0 on passenger duty in Greece; No LB 958, simmering in the heat at Philadelphia, near Thessalonika on 3 June 1964 with train No 502. The 16 engines were Class LB Nos 951-959 (WD Nos 73652-73660 respectively) and 960-966 (WD Nos 73672/4/7/8/82/3/4 respectively.)/*David Dixon*

The principal dimensions of the 2-10-0 engines were as follows: two cylinders 19in by 28in; coupled wheels 4ft 8½in diameter; boiler pressure 225lb psi; tube heating surfaces 1759sq ft; firebox heating surface 178sq ft; superheater heating surface 423sq ft; grate area 40sq ft. Tractive effort at 85 per cent boiler pressure was 34 215lb, the same as for the 2-8-0.

More orthodox lagging was used for the big boiler. Beneath the steel plates, clothing the boiler, were asbestos mattresses, laid against the barrel and the firebox. As in the case of the 2-8-0s, both Westinghouse and vacuum brakes were fitted for train use, whilst the engine had the steam brake. No brake blocks were fitted to the trailing coupled wheels. Steam sanding gear was provided ahead of the leading coupled wheels and to both sides of the driving wheels.

The engines were built as follows:

Nos 3650- 3749	North British	1943/4
Nos 73750-73799	North British	1945

With the addition of 70000 to all WD numbers in September 1944, the final 50 engines were all turned out with five figure numbers and the earlier ones quickly brought into line.

The engines were put to work in Britain until needed overseas but, in the event, Nos 73651 and 73774-73799 never left Britain. In 1944 20 were despatched to the Middle East Forces and in 1944/5 there were 43 in Belgium and 60 in Holland; by June 1946 all these 103 were in Holland. This left 20 in the Middle East and 20 on the LNER, with the other seven, in WD hands. Eventually 25 were taken into BR stock, leaving two in WD ownership.

When the big 2-10-0s first appeared, and were running-in on British main lines, they aroused a good deal of interest in railway circles. Their subsequent success influenced Riddles when planning the standard BR Class 9F heavy freight engines, and the same wheel arrangement was used in favour of an earlier proposal for a 2-8-2 design, as discussed on page 98.

First of class withdrawn: 90753/4 (1961)*
Last of class withdrawn: 90773 (1962)*
Examples preserved: AD600 (ex WD 73651)
WD 73755 *Longmoor*

* These were the first and last on the BR stocklist, but at the time of writing it was possible that examples of the class were still intact in Greece and Syria, although probably no longer steamed regularly.

Top left: The Longmoor Military Railway retained two of the WD 2-10-0s for Army use, after the return to peacetime in Europe. These were Nos 73651 and 73797, later becoming Nos WD (later AD) 600/1 respectively. Finished in the bright blue livery of the Longmoor system in its later years, with red lining-out on the cab, cylinders and tender, No WD 601 *Kitchener* makes an attractive picture, standing in the works yard at Eastleigh on 20 September 1963, following a general overhaul. The engine was fitted with an additional air compressor on the smokebox side, and had been altered to oil-firing. Steam turbo-generator for the large electric headlight visible on running plate at front left-hand side./*H. Wheeler*

Bottom Left: The other Longmoor 2-10-0, No AD 600 (formerly No 73651) *Gordon,* seen working an RCTS Longmoor Railtour special over Southern Region metals, on the 1 in 80 gradient between Witley and Haslemere. Compared to the preceding picture of No 601, the engine was running as a coal-burner and did not carry the large electric headlight and turbo-generator. This engine has been preserved and is now on the Severn Valley Railway./*M. Pope*

Below: Withdrawal of the NS-owned 2-10-0s started in 1948 and by 1952 the last had gone, with the exception of No 73755 *Longmoor,* which was officially preserved and placed in the Dutch Railway Museum at Utrecht, after being restored to original WD livery and condition in 1954. The engine is seen on display, with a modern NS electric multiple-unit passing. All the engines working on the Dutch system had a tall extension added to the chimney, but this was evidently removed from No 73755, when preserved./*L. J. P. Albers*

Bottom: The four 2-10-0s in Syria were WD Nos 73685-73688, which became CFS (Chemins des Fer Syriens) Nos 150.685-150.688. These were the most up-to-date steam locomotives on the Syrian system, and still survived at the time of writing. With rakish smoke deflectors, huge electric headlights and other added details, No 150.688 was photographed at the head of the 'Taurus Express' at Aleppo, in 1971. The engine was painted in Desert Sand livery./*Jonathan Smith*

H. G. Ivatt

The Final Years of the LMS

In February 1946, H. G. Ivatt was appointed Chief Mechanical and Electrical Engineer of the LMS, following the unexpected death of C. E. Fairburn, who had succeeded Sir William Stanier. Ivatt remained as CME when the railways were nationalised in 1948, under the direction of the new Railway Executive, but he was then only responsible for London Midland Region locomotive affairs, and no longer had Scotland. When he retired in June 1951 he was the last of the four CMEs of the former Big Four railway companies to go, and the title of CME lapsed with his retirement.

2-6-0 Class 2F (later 2P/2F; 2MT) Mixed-Traffic Locomotives
Introduced: 1946
Total: 128
BR Power Class: 2

A modern small engine to replace some of the old Class 2 0-6-0s, dating from the pre-Grouping era, had been an acknowledged requirement for many years. The drawing office had produced all manner of engine diagrams in an attempt to please the motive power people, some of whom actually thought that construction of further Victoriana would suffice. During the second World War period, the somewhat depleted design staff under Coleman at Derby produced some interesting 'flights of fancy', as described in the Introduction on page 16, including 0-6-0s with bar frames, inside Walschaerts gear driven by outside return cranks, and an external style closely following the new 'Austerity' locomotives. Some of these proposals were for the Class 2 power category and some were for the larger Class 4. By 1944 Ivatt was able to impress upon all concerned that a 2-6-0 wheel arrangement was desirable and that the new lightweights (there was to be a twin 2-6-2T) would be of straightforward modern design, with the emphasis upon easy maintenance and operation. By the time the first example appeared, Ivatt had succeeded Fairburn as CME and their production design is rightly credited to Ivatt. The Class 2 engines were the first really modern small steam engines produced in Britain for many years and they soon proved to be ideal for branch

Below: LMS Class 2F 2-6-0 of 1946.

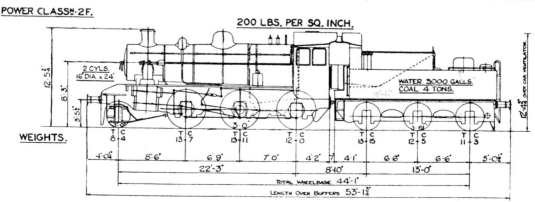

Top: Ivatt Class 2F 2-6-0 No 6415, built at Crewe in 1947 and illustrated in original LMS livery and condition, photographed at Bank Hall shed on 18 April 1950. Livery was plain black with straw colour lettering and numerals of sans-serif type, with a fine outline. Casing for fire irons on running-plate alongside the firebox, on right-hand side of engine, and large sandbox above centre and trailing coupled wheels./*H. C. Casserley*

Above: No 6419, last of the Ivatt Class 2 2-6-0s to appear under LMS ownership, and in that company's livery; built at Crewe in 1947. The engine was photographed on station pilot duty at Manchester Victoria. Ivatt's modified top feed design was placed well forward on boiler; Stanier pattern chimney as originally carried by the class (later replaced by BR castings); large sandbox on running plate alongside the Belpaire firebox./*W. S. Garth*

Above: Some improvement in the draughting for the Ivatt Class 2 engines was considered desirable, and an engine was sent to Swindon for tests in 1951; this was No 46413. Another engine, No 46424, had earlier received modified blastpipe dimensions at Derby and carried an ugly stovepipe chimney for the duration of these experiments, as seen here. Photographed shunting at Widnes on 26 April 1951./*H. C. Casserley*

Right: Unusual angle to view an Ivatt light Mogul, as No 46440 performs station pilot duties at Derby Midland on 31 August 1960. Modified casing to top feed; BR pattern chimney, and lined black mixed-traffic livery. The layout of sandboxes and mechanical lubricator on the running-plate is well illustrated. /*T. Boustead*

Far right: In 1950/1 Darlington commenced building Ivatt Class 2 2-6-0s for use on the Eastern and North Eastern Regions. Following the Swindon work on re-draughting a new, and very slender, chimney was provided, tapered outward from the base to the BR style rim, as seen here on No 46475. The engine has the battery box for BR AWS equipment immediately in front of the cab and has a small snowplough fitted. The builder's plates for these engines were LNE style brass ovals./*P. J. Sharpe*

line duties and other light work, whilst affording the enginemen a degree of comfort and efficiency sadly lacking in many of the asthmatic, aged, engines they replaced.

Except for the provision of a tender, the two Class 2 designs were practically identical. The principal dimensions, common to both the 2-6-0 and the 2-6-2T, were as follows: two cylinders 16in by 24in; coupled wheels 5ft 0in in diameter; boiler pressure 200lb psi; tube heating surfaces 924.5sq ft; firebox, 101.0sq ft; superheater, 134.0sq ft, and grate area 17.5sq ft. Tractive effort at 85per cent boiler pressure was 17 400lb.

Both types had self-cleaning smokeboxes, rocking grates, self-emptying ashpans, side-window cabs and outside Walschaerts valve gear. The tender for the 2-6-0 was fitted with a cab, and the coal bunker was inset to provide clear vision when running bunker-first. The tender capacity was 3000gal of water and 4ton of coal, and there was an iron ladder at the rear for ease of access to the tank top.

The new engines were extremely well received by the footplate and mechanical staff, and besides being good from the servicing viewpoint, they soon demonstrated a good turn of speed and snappy powers of acceleration, whilst being economical to run.

After nationalisation, tests at Swindon, in which No 46413 was compared with a Dean goods 0-6-0, revealed the possibilities of much improved draughting, and the class was then modified accordingly. A final batch to the Ivatt design was constructed at Swindon as late as 1953, following which the design was modified to incorporate BR standard fittings and became the standard Class 2 2-6-0 type, numbered in the 78000 series, as described in Section 12, on page 82. Prior to this the class had been built for use on the Eastern, North Eastern and Western Regions, as well as their home territory.

The engines were built as follows:

Nos 6400-6409	Crewe	1946
Nos 6410-6419	Crewe	1947
Nos 46420-46434	Crewe	1948
Nos 46435-46449	Crewe	1950
Nos 46450-46459	Crewe	1950
Nos 46460-46464	Crewe	1950
Nos 46465-46482	Darlington	1951
Nos 46483-46494	Darlington	1951
Nos 46495-46502	Darlington	1952
Nos 46503-46514	Swindon	1952
Nos 46515-46527	Swindon	1953

First of class withdrawn: 46407 (1961)
Last of class withdrawn: 46400/2/6/11/7/8/ 31-3/6/7/9/48/9/52/5/7/65/70/80/4-7/90-2/ 9/500-3/5/6/15/6/20/2/3. (1967)
Examples preserved: 46441/3/7/64.

Below: Evidently the very slender chimney design was disliked for its appearance — although performance was certainly improved! As a result, a new casting was made, in which the outside diameter of the chimney was increased considerably, to improve its looks. No 46491 sports this final version, which is throwing the exhaust high above the train, as the engine barks its way up the 1 in 62 to Troutbeck with the summer Saturdays only Workington-Manchester train./*P. Brock*

Top right: Also working the summer Saturdays-only Workington-Manchester train, over the former Cockermouth, Keswick & Penrith line, are two Ivatt Class 2 Moguls — No 46457 leading, the other unidentified — both working bunker-first. The excellent rear vision afforded by the inset coal bunker is well illustrated, also the ladder on the rear of the tender. BR 25kV warning flashes added to rear of tender and side of firebox./*P. Brock*

Bottom right: The final batches of Ivatt Moguls were built at Swindon in 1952/3 and were numbered 46503-46527, for use on the Western Region. No 46522 had been transferred to the LMR by the time this picture was taken at Bescot shed on 30 June 1963, but was in fully lined green livery, as favoured by Swindon in the later years of steam repairs for even the smallest types. These engines had GW-type top feed./*A. W. Martin*

SECTION 4

2-6-2T Class 2P (later 2P/2F; 2MT)
Mixed-Traffic Locomotives
Introduced: 1946
Total: 130
BR Power Class: 2

The twin of Ivatt's Class 2 2-6-0 was a small up-to-date 2-6-2T for light duties and this was practically identical, except for the provision of side tanks with a capacity of 1350gal and a short bunker, arranged to give clear vision, with a capacity for 3 tons of coal.

In the design development stage, whilst Fairburn was CME, a full-size wooden mock-up of the new 2-6-2T was constructed, to allow inspection and comment by shed staffs, in an attempt to avoid costly modifications once the new engines had actually been built and had entered service. The emphasis was upon ease of maintenance and servicing. The 2-6-2T had all the labour-saving devices fitted to the corresponding 2-6-0, and the principal dimensions were the same, as detailed on page 34.

These rather attractive little engines soon proved their worth, and were much appreciated by the LMS footplatemen and shed staffs. Like the 2-6-0, they benefited from the attentions of the Swindon tests and later ran with improved draughting. Further examples were constructed after nationalisation, including some for use on the Southern Region, and the design was then modified, to incorporate BR standard fittings,

and became the standard Class 2 2-6-2T numbered in the 84000 series, as described in Section 14, on page 88.

The engines were built as follows:

Nos	1200-1208	Crewe	1946
No	1209	Crewe	1947
Nos	41210-41229	Crewe	1948
Nos	41230-41259	Crewe	1949
Nos	41260-41289	Crewe	1950
Nos	41290-41299	Crewe	1951
Nos	41300-41319	Crewe	1952
Nos	41320-41329	Derby	1952

No 41272, built at Crewe in September 1950, had the distinction of being the 7000th locomotive erected there, and carried special commemorative plaques.

First of class withdrawn: 41235/6/46/7/52/ 4-9/63/5-7/9/71/7/8/80/8 (1962)
Last of class withdrawn: 41224/30/84/95, 41319/20 (1967)
Examples preserved: 41241/98, 41312/3

Below: LMS Class 2P 2-6-2T; introduced 1946

POWER CLASS 2P.

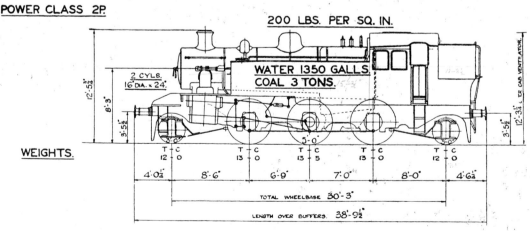

200 LBS. PER SQ. IN.

WATER 1350 GALLS.
COAL 3 TONS.

2 CYLS. 16" DIA. x 24".

WEIGHTS.

TOTAL WHEELBASE 30'-3"
LENGTH OVER BUFFERS 38'-9½"

1 in 128.2

Below: Class 2P 2-6-2T No 1200, first of the type built at Crewe in 1946, and seen here in works grey finish for photographic purposes. The sans-serif lettering and numerals were introduced by Ivatt with his new engines; livery was plain black. In practically every respect the 2-6-2T was indentical to the 2F 2-6-0. The sandbox for the trailing coupled wheels was located behind the cab footsteps, however. The tank fillers were at the leading end of the side tanks, on a portion which was slightly sloped to the front./*British Rail LMR*

Bottom: The design of the bunker on the light 2-6-2Ts was carefully planned, to afford good vision when running bunker-first or backing on to a train, as seen here on No 1206, which was photographed at Derby on 13 July 1947. The access ladder started well below the level of the bufferbeam and had two associated footsteps, one on the rear of the bunker and one on the side./*H. C. Casserley*

Above: Some of the Ivatt Class 2 2-6-2Ts were fitted with vacuum control gear for operating push-and-pull trains, as seen here on No 41273, photographed piloting a Compound 4-4-0 near Chinley, on a Manchester-Sheffield train, on 4 August 1951. Modified casing to the top feed, and Stanier pattern chimney./*J. D. Mills*

Top right: Swindon's improved blastpipe and chimney dimensions, developed as a result of trials with the Ivatt 2-6-0 No 46413, were also applied to the 2-6-2T version, with identical results. When Crewe built Nos 41290-41299 for use on the Southern Region, the new tapered narrow chimney was

applied, as seen on No 41294 photographed at Eastleigh on 1 June 1959. As in the case of the 2-6-0 (see page 37) there was some official dislike of the appearance of this chimney and it was subsequently redesigned, but a few engines retained the narrow version whilst on the SR./*C. P. Boocock*

Bottom right: Another push-and-pull fitted Ivatt 2-6-2T, No 41275, photographed leaving Aylesbury on a Cheddington train; passenger services were withdrawn from this branch in 1953. Such duties were light work for these engines, but the closure of many lines and the arrival of the diesel railcars displaced them whilst still comparatively new./*Ian Allan Library*

Top left: A real chimney oddity on 2-6-2T No 41214, seen working the very lightly loaded 3.3pm West Pennard-Evercreech Junction train, leaving West Pennard on 27 March 1965. The chimney rim is missing completely, producing a very odd appearance!/*B. J. Curl*

Bottom left: The Ivatt 2-6-2Ts operated by the Southern Region were often called upon to perform duties more in the scope of Class 4 engines, a challenge they met in gallant fashion, proving their remarkable capabilities for an engine of comparatively small dimensions. No 41291, with the narrow tapered chimney, was photographed leaving Victoria with the 10.7am train to Tunbridge Wells on 16 September 1957.
/*C. R. L. Coles*

Below: The sturdy final BR chimney casting, which replaced the tapered design, seen on Class 2 2-6-2T No 41296 as the engine left Evercreech Junction with the 5.0p.m. train to Highbridge on 30 March 1963./*J. D. Mills*

SECTION 5

2-6-0 Class 4F (later 4P/4F; 4MT) Mixed-Traffic Locomotives
Introduced: 1947
Total: 162
BR Power Class: 4

The final design produced by Ivatt, and the last new type to be introduced by the LMS prior to nationalisation, was the long-awaited answer to a need for a modern replacement for the very numerous 0-6-0 freight engines, including Fowler's standard type. As late as 1937-41, Stanier had approved the building of further engines to the Fowler design, and since then there had been various design proposals for modernised 0-6-0s, ranging from the simple expedient of placing a taper boiler upon the existing Fowler chassis, to an extremely ugly bar-frame design, with no footplate above the coupled wheels and with Allen's straight link valve gear. When the opportunity at last presented itself to finalise the design for production, Ivatt was able to insist upon the 2-6-0 wheel arrangement, as in the case of the lightweight Class 2 design.

In a number of respects the new Class 4 Mogul broke away from LMS convention, and from Ivatt's own first draft, which had shown an engine of very presentable appearance. In production form the design had echoes of the American S160 class 'Austerity' 2-8-0s, with the running plate high up, on the boiler flanks, completely exposing the wheels and frames.

This footplating was attached to the boiler flanks, instead of the frames, and the regulator was operated by external rodding along the boiler side from below the dome to the cab. The firebox was supported upon the frames by a single bracket at the bottom of the backplate. Everything about the new 2-6-0 was designed with ease of maintenance and

Below: LMS Class 4F 2-6-0 of 1947, in original condition, with double chimney as fitted to Nos 3000-3010, 43011-43049 when new.

Right: The very high footplate was attached to the boiler flank, completely exposing the wheels and valve gear. The external rodding to the regulator in the dome is clearly visible, also the arrangement of the reversing lever. No 3001 was photographed in Crewe works yard, in 1948. The huge double chimney is emphasised by comparing its dimensions with the gentleman at the front of the smokebox!/*Author's collection*

Below right: Third engine of the class, No 3002, built at Horwich in 1947 and finished in plain black LMS livery, with straw-coloured lettering and numerals. Photograph taken at Bletchley shed on 10 April 1948. The very austere appearance of the Ivatt Class 4 Moguls resulted from a desire to make maintenance and servicing as simple as possible, and the design had a number of features in common with American practice. The large double chimney had the twin exhaust outlets set outwards at an angle to each other, an arrangement which necessitated an extra long casting./*H. C. Casserley*

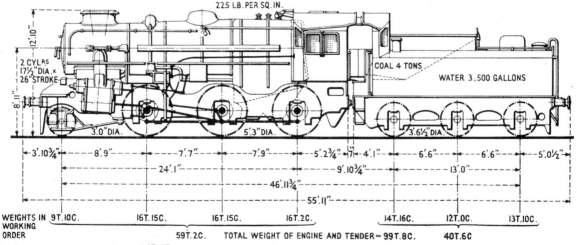

46

Above: Ivatt Class 4 2-6-0 No M3006, in early British Railways livery, before the adoption of the nationalised numbering scheme and insignia. The double exhaust arrangement proved inefficient as a steam-raiser and led to complaints when the engines were new — quite apart from less serious objections on the grounds of appearance!/*F. R. Hebron*

Centre right: Derby took in hand the steaming problems of the Ivatt Moguls and fitted a modified single blastpipe arrangement to No 43027, together with an ugly narrow stovepipe chimney. Trials with the engine led to the removal of the double blastpipes on all the engines which had them (Nos 43000-43049) and replacement by single blastpipe and chimney. Later, Swindon put one of the engines through its paces and further improvement in boiler output resulted. No 43027, with the experimental stovepipe affair, is seen inside Derby roundhouse on 26 April 1953./*H. C. Casserley*

Bottom right: In 1950 Doncaster commenced delivery of Ivatt Class 4 Moguls for use on the Eastern and North Eastern Regions. These were Nos 43050-43069 and were built new with single chimney and blastpipe, and finished in plain black BR livery. No 43061 was photographed at Doncaster, after major overhaul, on 10 April 1960. The tender has a recess for tablet catching apparatus, and a footstep added to the rear end. /*R. K. Evans*

operation in mind, and, like the smaller engines, it had self-cleaning smokebox, rocking grate and self-emptying ashpan. Outside Walschaerts valve gear was used, and the tender was fitted with a cab and had the coal bunker inset, to provide clear vision when running bunker-first.

The austere appearance of the new engine was crowned by a huge double chimney of unattractive shape, which seemed far too large for an engine of that size. This double chimney catered for a double exhaust in which the exit tips were not arranged vertically, as was normally the case, but were splayed outwards, at an angle to each other. In service this chimney and blastpipe arrangement soon proved to be far from satisfactory, due to incorrect proportions, and Derby produced a more satisfactory single chimney. Later, in 1951, Swindon put an example of the class under test, and considerable improvement was then achieved, with the excellent boiler at last draughted to obtain full output.

The principal dimensions were as follows: two cylinders 17½in diameter by 26in stroke; coupled wheels 5ft 3in diameter; boiler pressure 225lb psi; tube heating surfaces 1090sq ft; firebox 131sq ft; superheater 246.0sq ft; grate area 23.0sq ft. Tractive effort at 85 per cent boiler pressure was 24555lb.

The engines settled down to very satisfactory service, once the draughting problems were tackled, and the design was

Above: Darlington-built Ivatt Class 4 2-6-0 No 43106, last of the batch Nos 43070-43106 built there in 1950/1, and seen at Eastleigh works after overhaul in September 1965, with fully lined black BR livery. This engine was happily rescued from the scrap dealer's torch, and now operates on the Severn Valley line. Recess for tablet-catcher on tender, and 25kv warning signs applied./*G. Wheeler*

built at Darlington and Doncaster for use on the Eastern and North Eastern Regions, following nationalisation, and then further adapted to include the standard BR fittings, becoming the standard Class 4 2-6-0, in the 76000 series, as described in Section II, on page 78.

The engines were built as follows:

Nos	3000-3002	Horwich	1947
Nos	3003-3010	Horwich	1948
Nos	43011-43019	Horwich	1948
Nos	43020-43022	Horwich	1948
Nos	43023-43039	Horwich	1949
Nos	43040-43049	Horwich	1949

Nos 43050-43069	Doncaster	1950
Nos 43070-43096	Darlington	1950
Nos 43097-43106	Darlington	1951
Nos 43107-43111	Doncaster	1951
Nos 43112-43135	Horwich	1951
No 43136	Horwich	1952
Nos 43137-43155	Doncaster	1951
Nos 43156-43161	Doncaster	1952

First of class withdrawn: 43083/107/10/4/31/
42 (1963)
Last of class withdrawn: 43006/8/19/27/33
(1968)
Example preserved: 43106

Below: The well-proportioned single chimney certainly improved the otherwise basic appearance of Ivatt's Moguls, and gave them a more balanced front end. No 43137 was photographed in a superb setting, in July 1958, working a Glasgow (Queen St) to Perth train, composed of non-corridor stock. */W. J. V. Anderson*

Bottom: Humdrum duty for Class 4 2-6-0 No 43077, seen climbing the 1 in 50 out of Shipley towards Idle, with the daily Bradford-Idle freight, on 18 February 1967./*L. A. Nixon*

Above: A truly delightful study of Ivatt Mogul No 43121, trundling along the Langholm Branch with a minimal load, on 18 July 1967. Before Ivatt finalised the Mogul design there had been recurrent proposals simply to take the tanks off the Fairburn 2-6-4T design (see page 13) but this always fell down on the width across the cylinders, and the consequent lack of wide route availability./K. Hale

Below: Showing signs of wear, Ivatt Class 4 2-6-0 No 43013 double-heads the 12.15pm excursion train from Leicester to Alton Towers, with Stanier Class 5 4-6-0 No 45279, on Easter Monday 1963. The train is seen leaving the tunnel at Knighton North Junction and taking the Burton-on-Trent branch. The Mogul has BR AWS fitted, with protective plate behind the drawgear below the bufferbeam, and the tender has a steel guard at the rear of the bunker, as a protective measure when operating under the 25kV catenary, should footplate staff need to enter the coal space./G. D. King

R. A. Riddles

The BR Standard Locomotives

In January 1948 the main line railways of Great Britain were merged into a single national system, and all the design staffs and individual locomotive works were placed under the powerful control of R. A. Riddles, Member of the Railway Executive for Mechanical and Electrical Engineering. He instructed his team to examine the existing practices of each of the previous main line railways, with a view to selecting the best from each for future standards. These were incorporated in the design of a new range of standardised steam locomotives which were specifically intended to come within the limitations imposed by post-war operating conditions. These limitations included lower than ever standards in the quality of fuel, and, due to shortage of skilled staff, in both maintenance and firing. Steam traction was a filthy job and everything possible had to be done to make it more attractive; the emphasis was upon ease of maintenance and simplicity of operation. If it was impossible, at the time, materially to improve the existing conditions for the benefit of the locomotives, then the design of the locomotives had to be modified to meet the conditions.

Riddles knew what he wanted and conveyed his wishes to the Regional Chief Draughtsmen, via a committee chaired by E. S. Cox. His aims were set out under eight heads. These were: (1) the utmost in steam-producing capacity permitted by weight and clearance restrictions; (2) simplicity, visibility and accessibility, with the number of working parts reduced to a minimum; (3) proportions of all types of engine designed to give the widest possible range of mixed-traffic working; (4) increased life of bearings by the use of roller bearings for all wheels when financially justified, and otherwise of generously proportioned plain bearings with manganese liners; (5) simplification of shed maintenance by increased use of mechanical lubricators and grease lubrication; (6) reduction in disposal time at sheds by the fitting of self-cleaning smokeboxes, rocking grates, and self-emptying ashpans; (7) reduction to a minimum of slipping by the use of as high factors of adhesion as possible, and

of sensitive regulators and efficient sanding gear; and (8) within the foregoing requirements, the promotion of maximum thermal efficiency by large firegrate areas, to assure low rates of combustion in average working conditions, coupled with long-lap valve gear and high temperature superheat.

For the new designs the use of two cylinders only was decided upon for the following reasons: (1) to attain the ultimate in simplicity and accessibility; (2) the split inside big-end could be a source of trouble; (3) a built-up crank axle was expensive, both in first cost and maintenance, and (4) other things being equal, four exhausts per revolution promoted better steaming than did six, or eight.

The various inter-Regional committees had assembled enough data, together with the results of the 1948 Locomotive Exchange Trials, by the early months of 1949 for work to start on the new BR standard designs. The work had necessarily to be divided between the headquarters drawing offices of the previous four main line companies, namely Brighton, Derby, Doncaster and Swindon, but instead of allocating a complete locomotive to any one office, each of the four was made responsible for preparation of standard drawings for particular components in respect of all the engine types, as follows:

Brighton: Brakes and sanding gear.
Derby: Bogies and trucks; tenders; wheels; tyres; axles and spring gear.
Doncaster: Coupling and connecting rods; valve gear and cylinder details.
Swindon: Boiler and smokebox details; steam fittings.

In addition, each drawing office was designated 'parent' for one or more of the standard types, with the responsibility of making the general arrangement drawings. Under the guidance of E. S. Cox, for the new Riddles standard locomotives, a remarkable unity of style and detail design was achieved,, and a strong family likeness was carried by all the twelve standard locomotive classes, of which 999 were built, up to the close of the steam era on British Railways.

The descriptions of each class, in the sections that follow, are listed in the order of year of first introduction of the class to traffic.

SECTION 6

4-6-2 Class 7 70000
Mixed-Traffic Locomotives
Introduced: 1951
Total: 55
'Britannias'

When the first standard BR locomotive, No 70000 *Britannia* made its debut in January 1951, few people could have imagined that it had ahead of it a working life of only 16 years and that a representative of the same class would have the doubtful distinction of hauling the last BR steam train over part of its journey. Nevertheless, the problems of post-war steam operation and maintenance, which in time led to the change to diesel and electric traction, were well to fore in the design team's minds when the new standard engines were being developed, and their finalised form and appearance was largely dictated by the need for simplicity, good accessibility and reduction in costs and time required for servicing and maintenance.

The Class 7 Pacific was intended as a fast mixed-traffic engine with wide route availability, roughly equal in power to existing types such as the WR 'Castle' class 4-6-0, the London Midland rebuilt 'Royal Scot' 4-6-0, the SR 'West Country' Pacific and the Eastern Region V2 2-6-2. The most significant difference lay in the use of only two cylinders, plus a large boiler with wide firebox, whereas all the afore-mentioned types had three or more cylinders. Everything about the design was as functional in layout as possible, with a cross-blend of American and Continental features evident in the finalised appearance, but with a true touch of British refinement in the detailing which somehow produced a handsome and well-balanced design, despite all the exposed piping and the high running plate.

The mixed-traffic designation was evident in the use of coupled wheels of only 6ft 2in diameter, but the 'Britannias' proved themselves quite capable of maintaining express passenger speeds and schedules, the smaller wheels proving to be no detriment. The use of a single blastpipe and chimney was a surprise at the time, when many large engines were fitted with double, or multiple, blastpipes, but again, this feature did not impair their performance in any significant way. The use of only two cylinders, of 20in diameter by 28in stroke, certainly reduced repair time and costs compared to multi-cylinder engines, and also reduced the initial capital cost per engine. Other features in the design included generous provision of washout plugs and doors, improved design of regulator in the smokebox, improved accessibility of injectors, pipes and pipework, and better cab and tender layout. A wooden mock-up of the proposed cab was exhibited to staff before the design was finalised. The reversing gear had an end-on wheel connected to a long cardan shaft running

Below: BR Standard Class 7 4-6-2, with type BR1A tender attached. The boiler was type BR1. Parent office for the design was Derby. Total weight of engine and tender with type BR1A tender attached was 146tons 10cwt.

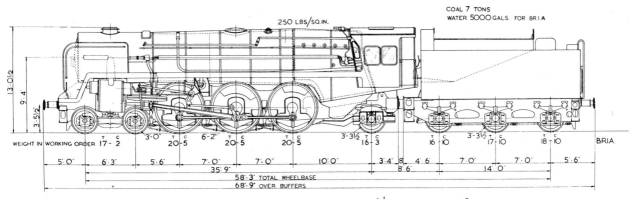

250 LBS/SQ.IN.

COAL 7 TONS
WATER 5000 GALS. FOR BR.I.A

WEIGHT IN WORKING ORDER 17 - 2

MINIMUM RADIUS CURVE WITHOUT GAUGE WIDENING 6 CHAINS (4½ CHAINS DEAD SLOW)

Top: Standing outside the Crewe paint shop and displaying the skills of the painter to perfection, No 70000 *Britannia* is seen ready to head south for the naming ceremony at Marylebone (which was on 30 January 1951) with bright metal finish to the wheel rims, handrails, buffers and drawgear. Livery was BR passenger green with orange and black lining, and a red background to the namplate. This shows the as-built condition of the first engine, with very small flat dome cover, and hollow axles on coupled wheels. No draught screens were fitted between engine and tender. In the original cab design, seen here, the entire footplate was an extension of the cab floor backwards to the front face of the tender; there was no fallplate. This floor was supported by cantilever brackets on the firebox./*British Rail LMR*

Above: The second standard Class 7 Pacific, No 70001 *Lord Hurcomb*, entering Liverpool Street station on 1 March 1951 at the head of the up 'Hook Continental', with the engine still in the original state, with flat dome and hollow coupled wheel axles. In the first months of service some teething troubles were experienced with the new design. There was some cylinder damage, due to carry-over of water from the dome. The design of the dome was modified and a larger casing was fitted. The coupled wheels shifted on their hollow axles, on some engines, causing damage to the valve motion. Throughout November 1951, all the 25 engines so far built were temporarily withdrawn from service for modification, but all were back in service by early 1952, with the hollow axle ends plugged. /*R. E. Vincent*

Above: Of the 25 'Britannias' scheduled for the 1951 building programme, the first 15 were allocated to the Eastern Region and the next 10 for the Western, but some changes were made in order to show-off the new engines; Nos 70009/14 were sent on loan to the Southern, whilst the London Midland Region received Nos 70015/16 which were intended for the Western. The Southern also received No 70004, once the Festival of Britain exhibition had ended, and this engine was kept-up in the special finish for use on the 'Golden Arrow'. The 'Bournemouth Belle' was another prestige train which was 'Britannia'-hauled at the time, and No 70009 *Alfred the Great* was photographed with this heavy Pullman car load at Battledown Flyover on 4 August 1951. A further transfer of 'Britannias' to the SR took place in 1953, when 10 of the WR allocation were on loan to replace the 'Merchant Navy'. Pacifics, which had been temporarily withdrawn from service./*E. D. Bruton*

Below: For the 1951 Festival of Britain exhibition, held on the South Bank of the Thames, close to Waterloo station, 'Britannia' Pacific No 70004 *William Shakespeare* was delivered new from Crewe with a special exhibition finish. This close-up of the front end of the engine, taken whilst on show, gives some idea of how beautifully groomed it was, and shows details such as the steam-operated cylinder drain cocks; triple slidebars and slipper crosshead and link drive to mechanical lubricator within the running angle./*British Rail SR*

Above: In the mid-1950s comparative trials of air-brake and vacuum brake equipment were held by British Railways, in an attempt to settle the debate for future standardisation. Two of the 1953-built 'Britannia' Pacifics were delivered new with dual braking. The Westinghouse air brake compressors were prominently sited at the front of the engine, and prevented the use of smoke deflectors. Nos 70043/4 were used for mineral train trials on the Midland main line, as well as normal express passenger working. Nos 70043/4 were later returned to normal, with the Westinghouse brake equipment removed, and smoke deflectors added; they then received their allotted names. No 70044 (later *Earl Haig*) was photographed at Euston station having just worked the up 'Mancunian' express. */P. Ransome-Wallis*

Centre right: The new two-cylinder Pacifics had been extremely well received on the Great Eastern line, when first introduced, and had transformed that line's timetable and quality of service. But when the first of the next batch of engines was allocated to the Western Region the enginemen's reactions were very different! Eight engines were delivered in the summer of 1951, four to Old Oak Common and two each to Laira and Newton Abbot. There was some foundation for the WR dislike, but once prejudice had been overcome and all the engines had been allocated to Cardiff (Canton) they proved themselves on Western metals, at least so far as the South Wales express turns were concerned. No 70022 *Tornado,* of the first WR batch (Nos 70017-70024), was photographed when brand new, at Bristol Temple Meads with the 11.55am Manchester (London Road)-Plymouth train on 15 September 1951. The second batch for the WR had type BR1A tenders with an increased water capacity of 5000gal; externally they resembled the type BR1./*J. D. Mills*

Above: The smoke deflectors on some WR-allocated 'Britannia' Pacifics were modified in an attempt to improve the driver's forward vision. This followed the accident at Milton, near Didcot in 1955 when No 70026 *Polar Star* was derailed, with eleven persons killed and 150 injured, whilst working an up excursion train from South Wales. The handrails were removed from the deflectors and six handholds were cut into the plates, with brass edging, as seen here on No 70016 *Ariel.* The ejector pipe was relocated at the smokebox end, further to improve the driver's vision. Rubber bellows are prominent in this picture, between cab and tender, to reduce draughts. Photographed at Swindon on 1 September 1957./*A. W. Martin*

Bottom left: Progressive improvements and modifications were made to the 'Britannias' as each new batch was produced. The final 10 engines had type BR1D tenders and modified cabs; the latter in an attempt to reduce draughts. The larger tenders held 9tons of coal and 4725gal of water, had flush sides with curved tops and were fitted with a steam-operated coal pusher. Total weight in working order of the 'Britannias' fitted with these tenders was increased to 148tons 10cwt, compared to 141tons 4cwt for the BR1 tender and engine. No 70046 was photographed at Newton Heath shed in June 1959 and prior to receiving nameplates (later *Anzac*). No 70047 of this batch was the only 'Britannia' Pacific never named, for some unknown reason. Detail alterations visible include raised sandbox fillers; solid axles on coupled wheels and tapered rectangular section coupling rods. Speedometer drive from rear coupled crankpin. /*J. E. Wilkinson*

forward from the cab, with the screw mounted on the forward end and acting directly on the weigh-shaft arm.

The principal dimensions of the 'Britannia' Pacifics were as follows: two cylinders 20in by 28in; coupled wheels 6ft 2in; boiler pressure 250lb psi; tube heating surfaces 1286sq ft; firebox heating surface 210sq ft; superheater heating surface 704sq ft (reduced to 677sq ft in Nos 70045-70054 by shortening of elements;) grate area 42sq ft. Tractive effort was 32 150lb at 85 per cent boiler pressure.

The engines were built as follows:

Nos 70000-70024	Crewe	1951
Nos 70025-70044	Crewe	1952/3
Nos 70045-70054	Crewe	1954

The various batches were allocated to the following Regions for operating purposes: Nos 70000-70014, Eastern; Nos 70015-70024, Western; Nos 70025-70029, Western; Nos 70030-70044, London Midland; Nos 70045-70049, London Midland; and Nos 70050-70054 Scottish. In practice some alterations took place with additional engines going to the Eastern Region, and three going to the Southern for a time. All the engines were allocated to the London Midland for maintenance purposes.

Detail differences in the batches included Nos 70035-70039 with roller bearings on driving wheels only; Nos 70040-70049 with plain boxes on all coupled wheels; Nos 70024-70029 type BR1A tenders with 5000 gallon water capacity and 7 tons of coal; and

57

Nos 70045-70054 with flush-sided type BRID tenders with steam-operated coal pushers and a capacity of 4725 gallons and 9 tons of coal. The BRID tenders weighed 54.5 tons when full, and the handrail from cab roof to back end of footplate was abolished, with a grab rail substituted at the front end of tender, to waist height only.

Generally speaking the 'Britannias' lived up to their designers' expectations, once various teething troubles had been overcome, but they were better received on some Regions than on others. The Western, in particular, took an early dislike to them, only overcome when all their allocation was centred on one shed. This dislike was due to unfamiliarity with many of the design features, compared to their existing Swindon engines. In the hands of keen enginemen, who had taken the trouble to learn how best to handle them, the two-cylinder Pacifics could perform in a manner more akin to multi-cylinder Class 8 steam power, and frequently did.

One problem experienced, when the class was new, was a pronounced fore-and-aft motion imparted by the 'Britannias' (and other new standard tender engines) to their trains. This was no new problem with two-cylinder engines, and in this case was solved by modification to the tender drawbar spring. The crews complained that the cabs were draughty; measures were taken to rectify this,

Above: The last ten engines built were originally allocated to the London Midland and Scottish Regions, and their larger tender capacity enabled them to be used on the longer express duties, including the North Wales route, with trains such as the 'Irish Mail', seen here in the charge of No 70045 *Lord Rowallan*. A detail alteration clearly visible in this view is the large footstep added below the smokebox, between the frames./*British Rail LMR*

Top right: No 70037 *Hereward The Wake*, one of the second batch of 20 engines, completed in 1952/3, with modified wheel balancing, improved cab-tender drawbar and rectangular section coupling rods. The picture was taken after the engine had received modified grab rails and hand holds on the smoke deflector plates, a rather neater form than that applied by Swindon (see page 57). The BR AWS battery box is also seen, located on the running plate just in front of the firebox. The type BR1 tender had a large footblock added to the rear end on each side, on the tank top, to assist water-filling operations./*P. Ransome-Wallis*

Right: 'Britannia' Pacific No 70028 (formerly *Royal Star*) at the head of a Crewe-Carlisle freight, near Leyland on 2 September 1966, one year before withdrawal for scrap. The engine is in the economy plain green livery latterly applied to steam by Crewe Works, and has had the smokebox numberplate, shed plate and nameplates removed for safe keeping. Top lampbracket lowered to centre left of smokebox door./*K. J. Meek*

Left: Comparison with the following picture of No 70001 clearly shows the revised cab/tender arrangement adopted for later standard engines, with a short fallplate reintroduced. These modifications were made to improve cab comfort and reduce noise and draughts, which had been a source of complaint from footplatemen on the first engines. The trailing truck had laminated springing, which gave rise to complaints of hard riding. No 70045 *Lord Rowallan* was photographed in close-up at Liverpool Exchange on 1 September 1967 in plain green livery. The small bracket of the cabside had been intended to display the name of the driver, relic of a short-lived scheme on the LMR in the 1950s./*P. Gerald*

Below: Minus nameplates, in plain green economy livery and decidedly grubby, No 70001 (formerly *Lord Hurcomb*) makes an interesting comparison with the pictured reproduced on page 54. The 'Britannias' arrived late on the British locomotive scene, and inevitably suffered from the general decline in standards of maintenance, in the transitional period of change to diesel and electric traction. No 70001 was photogtraphed leaving Bradford (Forster Square) on the 3.40pm slow to Carlisle, in April 1966. It was withdrawn from service just four months later. /*J. S. Whiteley*

Right: Temporarily back on Southern Region metals, 'Britannia' Pacific No 70004 (formerly *William Shakespeare*), once the pride of Stewarts Lane shed, seen at the head of the 5.23pm Waterloo-Southampton Docks 'Ocean Liner Express' on 16 August 1966. The engine was on the SR for railtour purposes and had been repainted (unofficially) in a lighter than normal shade of green. No nameplates, but still in remarkably good condition, and still with handrails on smoke deflectors, and fluted coupling rods./*Brian Stephenson*

and some improvement would have been made to the very hard-riding characteristics of the trailing truck, if construction had continued.

On the Great Eastern main line the class positively shone; on the SR 'Golden Arrow' they achieved prestige; on the London Midland and Scottish Regions they performed some of their best work but also their final and most humdrum duties, with the last two or three years witnessing a sad spectacle of dirty and neglected steam power which had years of life left in it when scrapped. They certainly deserved a better fate; they were splendid machines.

First of class withdrawn: 70007/44 (1965)
Last of class withdrawn: 70004/11/2/4/ 21-25/35/45/9/51 (1967)
Examples preserved: 70000/13.

Below: The original intention to officially preserve No 70000 *Britannia* was dropped by the British Railways Board in favour of No 70013 *Oliver Cromwell*, following vandalism of the first engine whilst in store. No 70013 was taken in Crewe works for a major overhaul in January 1967 and fully repainted, with a view to further operation until the end of steam; then preservation. She was the last steam locomotive overhauled at Crewe for BR use and a small ceremony took place on 2 February 1967 when the engine was returned to traffic. A period of railtour and special train workings followed, culminating with the engine working one leg of the final BR steam special, over the section from Manchester-Carlisle on 11 August 1968. Immediately afterwards the engine was sent to Bressingham Steam Museum, Diss, for permanent preservation and occasional steaming. No 70013 was photographed at Appleby on the Settle and Carlisle line, returning light engine from Carlisle to Lostock Hall shed, after taking part in the final steam run. This view shows the BR1 tender detail, with the additional footblocks on the rear end./*Mrs. E. Cross*

SECTION 7

4-6-2 Class 6 72000
Mixed-Traffic Locomotives
Introduced: 1951
Total: 10
'Clans'

Of the twelve standard locomotive types in the BR power range, the Class 6 Pacific was to prove the least effective, and only 10 engines were constructed, although more were at one stage envisaged. The design was basically the same as the very successful Class 7 'Britannia' Pacific, but with a somewhat smaller boiler and cylinders. In everyday service they fell a little short of expectations, with the excellent Class 5 4-6-0 almost equal in performance capacity, and the 'Britannia' a much stronger engine all round.

The Class 6 Pacific was intended for use on routes on which axle load restrictions prevented the use of the larger Class 7. The smaller boiler was carried on the same chassis as the Class 7 and the maximum axle load was 19tons in full working order, compared to 20tons 5cwt for the larger engine. The tender was indentical to the type BRI fitted to the first batch of 'Britannias', with a water capacity of 4250gal and 7tons of coal.

Below: Standard BR Class 6 4-6-2. The boiler was type BR2. Parent office for the design was Derby. Total weight of engine and tender in full working order (with type BR1 tender) was 137tons 13cwt.

The principal dimensions were as follows: two cylinders 19½in by 28in; boiler pressure 225lb psi; coupled wheels 6ft 2in diameter; tube heating surfaces 1878sq ft; firebox heating surface 195sq ft; superheater 592sq ft; grate area 36sq ft. Tractive effort at 85per cent boiler pressure was 27 250 lb.

The engines were built as follows:

Nos 72000-72009   Crewe   1951/2

A further 15 engines were included in the 1952 building programme, for construction at Crewe, but the order was subsequently cancelled. These would have been Nos 72010-72014 for the Southern Region and 72015-72024 for the Scottish Region. The London Midland Region was responsible for maintenance of the engines built, which were allocated to the Scottish Region for operating purposes.

The ten 'Clan' Pacifics were well liked by their enginemen, but at first showed a certain shyness for steam, whilst their adhesive weight of 56tons 18cwt did not compare too favourably with the 60tons of the Stanier 'Jubilee' class 4-6-0s which then performed similar duties. Although allocated to the Scottish Region the 'Clans' were not used over the difficult Highland Line, but instead spent much of their time on the Glasgow-Liverpool and Manchester workings. Riddles is on record as believing, with hindsight, that a 4-8-0 wheel arrangement would have produced a more useful engine, with an adhesive weight of some 72tons, which would have been ideal for the difficult Scottish routes. Engines of the class were tried out on the Midland main line,

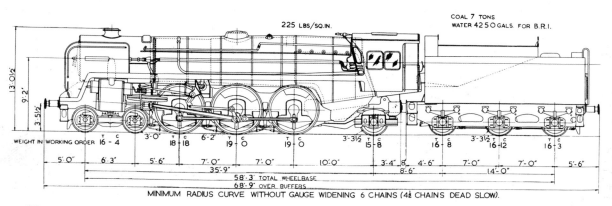

and on the Great Eastern run to Ipswich and Norwich, but no further orders were placed as in both cases the larger 'Britannias' were obviously more effective, whilst some people thought the Class 5 4-6-0 would suffice. Dieselisation ended the debate!

First of class withdrawn: 72000/1/2/3/4 (1962)
Last of class withdrawn: 72006 (1966)
None preserved

Below: Standard Class 6 Pacific No 72002 *Clan Campbell* storms up Beattock with a Birmingham-Glasgow working in April 1953. The 10 engines of the class spent most of their time on Glasgow-Manchester, Liverpool and Birmingham trains, instead of the routes north of Glasgow, and as a solution to motive power needs on the difficult Highland line they were not ideal, being lower in adhesive power than was desirable. /P. Ransome-Wallis

Top left: Photographed at Polmadie shed, Glasgow, soon after delivery from Crewe; 'Clan' Pacific No 72001 *Clan Cameron.* Chime whistle located on boiler side; cutaway in running angle of footplating for mechanical lubricator. Except for the smaller boiler, and large boiler mountings, the class was virtually identical in appearance to the larger Class 7 'Britannia' Pacifics, but the taller chimney gave these engines a rakish look. No draught screens fitted between engine cab and tender when this picture was taken./*Ian Allan Library*

Bottom left: Clan MacIntosh, photographed standing in Lancaster Old goods yard on 23 May 1964. Since building in 1952, No 72007 had scarcely altered in appearance except for the addition of BR AWS gear with the battery box located on the running plate just ahead of the firebox. The chime whistle had been replaced by a standard BR whistle, still located on the

boiler side. The cab carried the 6MT power classification favoured for a while, and the copper piping on the firebox side had been scraped and burnished./*J. Davenport*

Below: In the final phase of steam operations on BR, numerous railtours were arranged using motive power not normally found on the lines to be covered. A typical example, for the Home Counties Railway Society, made use of a Scottish Region 'Clan' Pacific over Western Region metals from Paddington to Swindon on 8 December 1963. Class 6 No 72006 *Clan MacKenzie* was the engine chosen, and is seen, at the head of the special train, passing Hayes & Harlington in the chill morning mist. The tender had the large footblock added to the rear of the tank top, and the canvas draught screens were fitted between cab and tender./*Brian Stephenson*

SECTION 8

4-6-0 Class 5 73000
Mixed-Traffic Locomotives
Introduced: 1951
Total: 172

In the draft proposals for new standard BR locomotives the Class 5 power category was envisaged as a Pacific, with an 18ton axle load, two cylinders 19½in by 28in and 225lb psi boiler pressure and a wide grate with an area of 36 sq ft. This would have had bar frames and a double chimney and blastpipe. As work progressed this scheme gave way to a 4-6-0, using certain parts in common with the larger Class 6 Pacific, but with the excellent boiler design of the Stanier LMS Class 5 4-6-0, as developed by Ivatt.

The cylinders, valve gear and coupled wheels were the same as for the 'Clan' Pacifics, and the Class 5 engine carried the standard fittings on the boiler, with the Stanier top feed arrangement replaced by the the clack valves of SR type. The principal dimensions were as follows: two cylinders 19in diameter by 28in stroke; coupled wheels 6ft 2in diameter; boiler pressure 225lb psi; tube heating surfaces 1479 sq ft; firebox heating surface 171sq ft; superheater heating surface 358sq ft; grate area 28.7sq ft. Tractive effort at 85 per cent boiler pressure was 26 120lb.

The engines were built as follows:

Nos 73000-73004	Derby	1951
Nos 73005-73009	Derby	1951
Nos 73010-73029	Derby	1951/2
Nos 73030-73039	Derby	1952/3
Nos 73040-73049	Derby	1953
Nos 73050-73052	Derby	1954
Nos 73053-73054	Derby	1954
Nos 73055-73064	Derby	1954
Nos 73065-73074	Derby	1954
Nos 73075-73079	Derby	1955
Nos 73080-73089	Derby	1955
Nos 73090-73099	Derby	1955
Nos 73100-73109	Doncaster	1955/6
Nos 73110-73119	Doncaster	1955
Nos 73120-73124	Doncaster	1956
Nos 73125-73134	Derby	1956
Nos 73135-73144	Derby	1956
Nos 73145-73154	Derby	1957
Nos 73155-73159	Doncaster	1956/7
Nos 73160-73171	Doncaster	1957

When new, the engines were allocated to the following Regions for operating purposes (the same Region was responsible for maintenance, in each case):

London Midland Region: Nos 73000-73004; 73010-73029; 73040-73049; 73053-73054; 73065-73074; 73090-73099; 73135-73144.
Scottish Region: Nos 73005-73009; 73030-73039; 73055-73064; 73075-73079; 73100-73109; 73120-73124; 73145-73154.
Southern Region: Nos 73050-73052; 73080-73089; 73110-73119.
Western Region: Nos 73125-73134.
Eastern/North Eastern Regions: Nos 73155-73159; 73160-73171.

The successive batches had various detail differences, in particular the type of tender

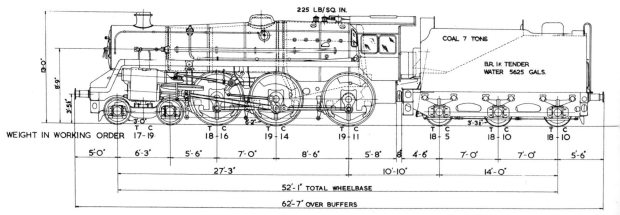

66

Left: Standard Class 5 4-6-0; later series for Southern Region with type BR1F tender fitted and modified cab with fallplate reintroduced. Whistle relocated on top of firebox. The boiler was type BR3. Total weight of engine and type BR1F tender in full working order was 131tons 5cwt; or 125tons 3cwt with the type BR1 tender. Parent office for the design was Doncaster.

Top: Shortly after completion at Derby works, the first of the new standard Class 5 4-6-0s was sent to Marylebone for official inspection and was exhibited to the technical press. The engine is seen at Neasden shed on 26 April 1951 en route to Marylebone. Livery was black with LNWR style lining-out, and

on No 73000, as first delivered, there was only a single fine red line along the side of the running plate, from cab to bufferbeam. Chime whistle immediately behind chimney. Type BR1 tender fitted./*C. C. B. Herbert*

Above: The second engine of the class, No 73001, in brand new condition at Derby in April 1951. The livery had been altered to include full lining-out along the running plate angle from buffer beam to cab. No canvas draught screens between cab and tender; this feature was added soon afterwards following complaints of draughtiness from the footplatemen. Hollow axles on coupled wheels and I-section coupling rods./*T. Lakin*

67

Top right: Two engines, Nos 73030/1, were delivered fitted with Westinghouse brakes for the same series of fitted freight train trials on which 'Britannia' Pacifics Nos 70043/4 were used. Only one compressor, on the right-hand side of the smokebox, was fitted to the 4-6-0s, and the reservoir is visible below the running plate at the cab end. No 73030 was photographed on an up empty excursion stock train composed of former MR vehicles, near Radlett./*E. S. Cox*

Centre right: A Wolverhampton-Portsmouth excursion train near Eastleigh South on 26 September 1956. The engine was standard Class 5 4-6-0 No 73087, fitted with flush-sided, curved-top type BR1B tender with a capacity of 4725gal and 7tons of coal; fallplate reintroduced between tender and rear of cab, to reduce draughts. This engine was later named *Linette* by the Southern Region, after the 'King Arthur' class engine of that name had been withdrawn. Raised sandbox covers on running plate; plain section coupling rods; solid axles on coupled wheels./*L. Elsey*

Below: To increase their water capacity to 5625gal with 7tons of coal, the batch of Class 5 4-6-0s Nos 73110-73119 allocated to the SR Western section had large type BR1F tenders fitted (see diagram on page 66). No 73116 *Iseult* was photographed approaching Wilton with an eastbound express on 10 August 1963. The small 'King Arthur' type nameplate can be seen on the running plate angle above the driving wheel. BR AWS fitted, with protective shield behind front coupling. /*A Richardson*

attached, whilst Nos 73125-73154 had Caprotti valve gear. The tender variations were as follows: Type BRI, inset with a capacity of 4250gal and 7tons of coal, Nos 73000-73049 and 73053-73064; Type BRIA, with a capacity of 5000gal and 7tons of coal, inset, Nos 73050-73052; Type BRIB, flush sides, with a capacity of 4725gal and 7tons of coal, Nos 73080-73089, 73100-73109, 73120-73134; Type BRIC, flush sides, with a capacity of 4725gal and 9tons of coal, Nos 73065-73079, 73090-73099, 73135-73144; Type BRIF, high sided, with a capacity of 5625gal and 7tons of coal, Nos 73110-73119.

The class proved to be extremely reliable and popular, and were capable of putting up performances more in keeping with the larger Pacifics, when in good fettle. They were a worthy successor to the Stanier 'Black Fives' and the Caprotti engines proved to be particularly strong, which suggests that H. G. Ivatt's final version of the Stanier design was a move in the right direction at the time.

First of class withdrawn: 73027 (1964)
Last of class withdrawn: 73069 (1968)
Examples preserved: 73050*, 73082, 73129
* *No 73050 has now been named* City of Peterborough.

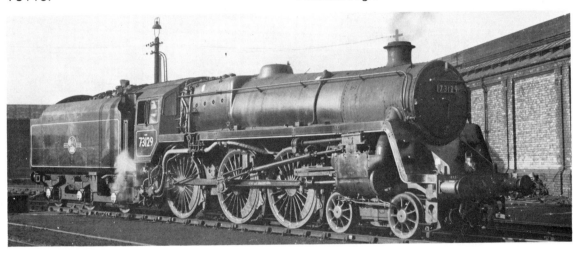

Above: Following the application of Caprotti valve gear to the Class 8 Pacific No 71000 (see page 90) it was decided to extend the use of this gear to gain further experience with it. Of the 47 Class 5 4-6-0s included in the 1956 building programme, 30 were selected for Caprotti gear, Nos 73125-73154. Photographed at Patricroft shed, No 73129 was attached to a type BR1B flush-sided tender. The whistle on later standard Class 5 4-6-0s was relocated on the top of the firebox immediately in front of the cab./*J. R. Carter*

Below: Photographed at Eastleigh, after a general repair, BR Standard Class 5 4-6-0 No 73014, resplendent in fully lined green livery, which was applied to only a few examples of the class. Since building, the engine had changed very little in appearance, except for replacement of chime whistle by normal BR type, located behind chimney, solid core axles on driving wheels; I-section coupling rods retained, and additional lampbrackets (for SR duties) on smokebox door; 25kv warning signs on front end, and side of firebox./*G Wheeler*

SECTION 9

4-6-0 Class 4 75000
Mixed-Traffic Locomotives
Introduced: 1951
Total: 80

One of the most popular of the standard classes, these versatile lightweight 4-6-0s could go practically anywhere and had a longer working range than their tank engine counterpart. Their low axle load enabled them to be used over routes where the larger Class 5 was prohibited, and as such they were similar in power and availability to the Western Region 7800 'Manor' class, but the L1 loading gauge allowed them to run over many lines from which the 'Manors' were banned due to their width over cylinders.

The design was derived from the Fairburn LMS 2-6-4T, and the boiler was evolved from the tank engine boiler by lengthening the barrel by 9in, retaining the same firebox dimensions. The use of a tender gave more fuel and water for the longer journeys.

The principal dimensions were as follows: two cylinders 18in by 28in; coupled wheels 5ft 8in diameter; boiler pressure 225lb psi; tube heating surfaces 1301sq ft; firebox heating surface 143sq ft; superheater heating surface 258sq ft; grate area 26.7sq ft. Tractive effort at 85 per cent boiler pressure was 25 515 lb. The maximum axle load was 17tons 5cwt.

The engines were built as follows:

Nos 75000-75009	Swindon	1951
Nos 75010-75019	Swindon	1951/2
Nos 75020-75029	Swindon	1952/3
Nos 75030-75049	Swindon	1953/4
Nos 75050-75064	Swindon	1955/6
Nos 75065-75079	Swindon	1956/7

A further order, for Nos 75080-75089, to have been built at Swindon for the Eastern Region, was cancelled.

When new, the engines were allocated to the following Regions for operating purposes (the Region responsible for maintenance is shown in brackets): Nos 75000-75009 Western Region (WR); Nos 75010-75019 London Midland Region (WR); Nos 75020-75029 Western Region (WR); Nos 75030-75049 London Midland Region (LMR); Nos 75050-75064 London Midland Region (LMR); Nos 75065-75079 Southern Region (WR). Later in their careers the class was maintained at Eastleigh.

First of class withdrawn: 75067 (1964)
Last of class withdrawn: 75048 (1968)
Examples preserved: 75027/9*/69/78

* Now named The Green Knight

Below: BR standard Class 4 4-6-0, with type BR2A tender attached. The boiler was type BR4. Parent office for the design was Brighton. Total weight in full working order, with type BR2A tender attached was 110tons 1cwt.

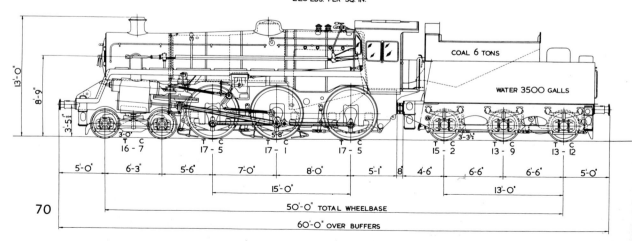

225 LBS. PER SQ. IN.

Below: In ex-works condition, BR Class 4 4-6-0 No 75019 was photographed at Eastleigh on 10 October 1965, still very much in original state, with I-section coupling rods and type BR2A inset tender. These rather well-proportioned and handsome engines were amongst the more effective BR standard types, and were used for the longer runs in the type 4 power category; having an excellent route availability./*G. Wheeler*

Bottom: Standard Class 4 4-6-0 makes a fine study pulling hard with a four-coach Preston-Wigan train, photographed passing Euxton Junction on 4 June 1960. Canvas draught screens between engine and tender clearly visible, showing their tendency to billow out. Large footblock added to rear of tender tank top./*J. E. Wilkinson*

Top: Some of the standard Class 4 4-6-0s on the Western Region, and all the engines allocated to the Southern Region, later received double blastpipes and chimneys, following draughting tests at Swindon. The double chimney produced by the WR for its locomotives was a huge and rather ugly casting as tall as the L1 loading gauge would permit, and certainly detracted from the appearance of the engines so fitted, as seen here on No 75029, photographed at Swindon, ex-works in fully lined passenger green livery./*L. King*

Above: Nos 75050-75079 were fitted with type BR1B tenders, with flush sides and a capacity of 7 tons of coal and 4725 gallons of water. No 75070 is seen, when new, working an Exeter-Plymouth local past Hemerdon signal box on 9 March 1956. Speedometer driven off rear coupled wheels, and plain section coupling rods fitted./*D. S. Fish*

Top right: The much neater double chimney casting produced by Eastleigh and fitted to all the Class 4 4-6-0s operating on the Southern Region, seen here on No 75074 at Eastleigh, ex-works in lined black livery. The double chimney and blastpipe improved the performance of these already very capable machines, and they were popular amongst enginemen on duties where the larger Class 5 was prohibited on account of axle load./*J. B. Bucknall*

Right: Still retaining the original single blastpipe and chimney, standard Class 4 No 75023, in grubby passenger green livery, pilots standard Class 5 4-6-0 No 73050 on the up 'Pines Express'. Photographed at Evercreech Junction on 16 September 1961. Orders for a further batch of ten Class 4 4-6-0s, for the Eastern Region were cancelled when dieselisation got under way and soon displaced steam from many of the duties this class regularly performed./*G. A. Richardson*

SECTION 10

2-6-4T Class 4 80000
Mixed-Traffic Locomotives
Introduced: 1951
Total: 155

The Fairburn LMS 2-6-4T design of 1945, which had been developed from Sir William Stanier's two-cylinder design of 1935, was at first considered for inclusion in the BR standard range in much the same form, modified only to include standard fittings. As in the case of the two lightweight Ivatt designs of 1946, the 2-6-0 and corresponding 2-6-2T, further examples of the Fairburn engines had been built since nationalisation, including a batch for the Southern Region (see Introduction, page 13).

On closer examination, it was realised that the design would require more drastic alterations if it was to be more widely used. In order to satisfy the universal L1 loading gauge it would be necessary to modify the cylinders and superstructure, and to use a higher boiler pressure. The 200lb psi of the Fairburn boiler called for cylinders of 19⅝in diameter by 26in stroke to produce the required tractive effort,

but the L1 loading gauge would only permit the use of 18in diameter cylinders. The boiler pressure was therefore raised to 225lb psi, which proved possible by retaining all the existing plates, but re-staying them at a closer pitch. The boiler fittings were altered to conform with the new BR standards, with boiler feed clack valves of Southern pattern in place of the LMS top feed, and with the rodding to the regulator in the dome, running externally from the cab.

For the standard Class 4 2-6-4Ts, the Brighton design office used a curved profile for the outer tank side sheets, and this, together with the raised footplating over the cylinders at the front end, resulted in an appearance quite distinct from the Fairburn engines. In common with the other new standard designs there was a return to the use of drop end footplating ahead of the cylinders, a feature absent on both Fairburn and Ivatt tank engines, and this considerably enhanced their looks.

Principal dimensions of the Class 4 2-6-4T engines were as follows: two cylinders 18in by 28in; coupled wheels 5ft 8in (compared to 5ft 9in for the LMS design); tube heating surfaces 1223sq ft; firebox heating surface 143sq ft, giving a total evaporative heating surface of 1366sq ft; superheater heating surface 240sq ft; grate area 26.7sq ft; boiler pressure 225lb psi and tractive effort 25 515lb at 85 per cent boiler pressure (compared to 24 670lb for the Fairburn design). Engine weight in full working order was 86tons 13cwt, compared to 85tons 5cwt, and the coal and water capacities

Below: Standard Class 4 2-6-4T. The boiler was classified type BR5. Parent office for the design was Brighton. Total weight in full working order was 86tons 13cwt.

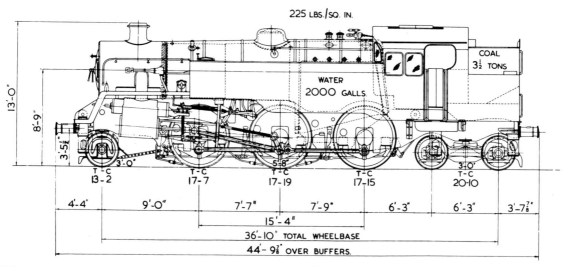

Above: In immaculate lined black livery, BR Class 4 2-6-4T No 80122 was photographed at Elgin on 20 April 1957. The raised footplating over the cylinders and the curved profile of the side tanks gave these engines a rakish look, compared to the Fairburn LMS design (see page 13) from which they were developed./*A. Cameron*

Below: Fresh from overhaul and the paint shop, No 80134 is seen with 25kV warning signs, BR AWS equipment, and speedometer. The engine was allocated to the Western Region at this time (87D shed) and the lampbrackets have been altered to GWR pattern./*J. B. Bucknall*

Above: Class 4 2-6-4T No 80001, of the batch of 10 built at Derby Works; photographed at Glasgow Central on a commuter working, complete with route indicator above the buffer-beam./*Eric Treacy*

remained the same, at 3½ tons and 2000gal respectively. An odd result of the re-designed side tanks was that it was discovered that although the designed capacity was 2000gal in each case, the rectangular tanks of the LMS engines were capable of carrying some 100gal in excess. Until this was pointed out it was eroneously believed that the BR standard 2-6-4Ts were heavier on water consumption!

The engines were built as follows:

Nos 80000-80009	Derby	1951
Nos 80010-80019	Brighton	1951/2
Nos 80020-80030	Brighton	1951/2
Nos 80031-80033	Brighton	1952
Nos 80034-80053	Brighton	1952
Nos 80054-80058	Derby	1954/5
Nos 80059-80068	Brighton	1953
Nos 80069-80080	Brighton	1953/4
Nos 80081-80095	Brighton	1954
Nos 80096-80105	Brighton	1954/5
Nos 80106-80115	Doncaster	1954
Nos 80116-80120	Brighton	1955
Nos 80121-80130	Brighton	1955
Nos 80131-80144	Brighton	1956
Nos 80145-80154	Brighton	1954/6

The original Regional allocations of the batches were as follows (Region responsible for maintenance shown in brackets):

Scottish Region (Sc.R): Nos 80000-80009, 80020-80030, 80054-80058, 80106-80115, 80121-80130.
Southern Region (SR): Nos 80010-80019, 80145-80154.
North Eastern Region (Sc.R): Nos 80031-80033.
London Midland Region (LMR): Nos 80034-80053, 80059-80068, 80081-80095.
Eastern Region (ENE): Nos 80069-80080, 80096-80105, 80116-80120, 80131-80144.

Like their Stanier forebears, the BR Class 4 2-6-4Ts proved to have an admirable turn of speed and good powers of acceleration. Electrification, and the suburban-type diesel railcars, displaced the engines from many of the commuter-type workings for which they were particularly well suited, and some ended their BR careers on humdrum duties. The popularity of the engines may perhaps be assessed from the fact that no less than ten were preserved, or scheduled for preservation, at the time of writing.

First of class withdrawn: 80103 (1962)
Last of class withdrawn: 80152 (1967)
Examples preserved: 80002/64/78*/9*/80*/98*/105/35/6*/51.

* *At Woodham's scrapyard Barry; pending preservation (1976)*

Above: No 80135 on the 'Cuckoo Line', working an Eastbourne-Tunbridge Wells train, and seen on the curve between Mayfield and the summit of the line, on a crisp February day. The BR standard 2-6-4Ts displaced the Brighton-built Fairburn LMS engines on SR territory, and the latter were transferred to other Regions. The second and third vehicles of the train are a pair of vintage LBSCR carriages, still in passenger service in the mid-1950s./*Derek Cross*

Below: Piloted by Stanier 8F 2-8-0 No 48706, standard Class 4 2-6-4T No 80043 makes a dashing sight at Templecombe (Lower) with a Stephenson Locomotive Society special train, over the Somerset and Dorset line, on 6 March 1966. /*Derek Cross*

SECTION 11

2-6-0 Class 4 76000
Mixed-Traffic Locomotives
Introduced: 1952
Total: 115

The BR standard Class 4 2-6-0 was the Ivatt LMS design of 1947, modified only to include the standard details, and with the benefits of the improvements in blastpipe and chimney proportions which had resulted from the Swindon tests on the original class. Visually, the standard engines were a considerable improvement upon Ivatt's austere and basic design; most of the rough edges were smoothed over, and the raised footplating was linked to the buffer beam level by a drop-end which tidied up the frontal aspect considerably.

The principal dimensions of the engines were as follows: two cylinders 17½in diameter by 26in stroke; coupled wheels 5ft 3in diameter; boiler pressure 225lb psi; tube heating surfaces 1075sq ft; firebox heating surface 131sq ft; superheater 247 sq ft; grate area 23sq ft. The tractive effort at 85 per cent boiler pressure was 24 170lb.

The engines were built as follows:

Nos 76000-76004	Horwich	1952
Nos 76005-76019	Horwich	1952/3
Nos 76020-76024	Doncaster	1952/3
Nos 76025-76029	Doncaster	1953
Nos 76030-76044	Doncaster	1953/4
Nos 76045-76052	Doncaster	1955/6
Nos 76053-76069	Doncaster	1955/6
Nos 76070-76074	Doncaster	1956
Nos 76075-76089	Horwich	1956/7
Nos 76090-76099	Horwich	1957
Nos 76100-76114	Doncaster	1957

When new, the various batches were allocated to the following Regions for operating purposes. The Region responsible for maintenance is shown in brackets, where it differed from the operating Region:

Scottish Region: Nos 76000-76004(ENE); 76070-76074 (ENE); 76090-76114.
Southern Region: Nos 76005-76019; 76025-76029; 76053-76069.
North Eastern Region: Nos 76020-76024 (ENE); 76045-76052 (ENE)
Eastern Region: Nos 76030-76044 (ENE).
London Midland Region: Nos 76075-76089.

The final engine of the class, No 76114, was the last new steam locomotive to be constructed at Doncaster works, in 1957.

First of class withdrawn: 76028 (1964)
Last of class withdrawn: 76084 (1967)
Examples preserved: 76017/79/84*

* No 76084 was still at Barry Scrapyard at the time of writing.

Below: Standard Class 4 2-6-0 engine, with type BR2A tender. Nos 76053-76069 were built with flush-sided tenders for use on the Southern Region; these carried 7 tons of coal and 4725gal of water, and were type BR1B. The boiler was classified type BR7. Parent office for the design was Doncaster. Total weight in full working order was 101 tons 18cwt, with type BR2A tender attached.

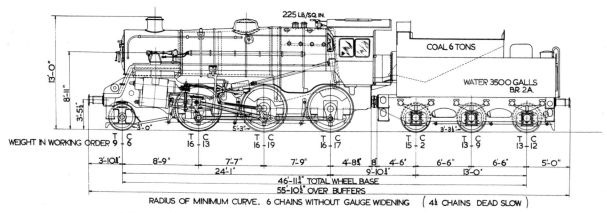

225 LB/SQ.IN.

COAL 6 TONS

WATER 3500 GALLS
BR. 2.A.

13'-0"

8'-11"

3'-5½"

WEIGHT IN WORKING ORDER 9 – 6 | T C | 16 – 13 | T C | 16 – 19 | T C | 16 – 17 | T C | 15 – 2 | T C | 13 – 9 | T C | 13 – 12 | T C

5'-0" | 5'-3"

3'-3½"

3'-10¾" | 8'-9" | 7'-7" | 7'-9" | 4'-8½" | 8 | 4'-6" | 6'-6" | 6'-6" | 5'-0"

24'-1" | 9'-10½" | 13'-0"

46'-11¾" TOTAL WHEEL BASE
55'-10½" OVER BUFFERS

RADIUS OF MINIMUM CURVE. 6 CHAINS WITHOUT GAUGE WIDENING   (4½ CHAINS DEAD SLOW)

1 in 134½

Above: Standard Class 4 2-6-0 No 76013 leaving Southampton with a Portsmouth-Salisbury train, composed of Western Region stock, on 5 September 1953./*P. Ransome-Wallis*

Below: No 76016, photographed at Eastleigh on 2 August 1955, showing the concertina draught screens fitted between engine and tender./*John Robertson*

Above: Tenders of type BR1B, with flush sides and a capacity of 7tons of coal and 4725gal of water, were attached to Nos 76053-76069, for use on the Southern Region. The layout of the cab footplate was modified to reduce draughts. No 76056 is seen, when new, hauling a light load on the Reading-Redhill cross country route, near Betchworth./*Ian Allan Library*

Top right: Standard Class 4 Mogul panned by the camera, with the 5ft 3in coupled wheels nicely blurred, on No 76066; seen passing Millbrook on an up freight in October 1966. This view illustrates the modified layout of the rear of the cab on later standard engines (see also page 60) and shows the 'daylight'

between boiler and frames, revealed by the high running plate./*John A. M. Vaughan*

Right: Riddles and Ivatt Class 4 Moguls in tandem, on a Saturdays-only South Shields-Blackpool train, at Kirkby Stephen East on 6 August 1960. The leading engine is BR Class 4 2-6-0 No 76024 and the Ivatt engine is No 43129. The picture provides a nice demonstration of how the appearance of two basically similar engines was modified by detail alterations and greater regard for aesthetic qualities. The original Ivatt design seems very angular compared to the BR version./*Derek Cross*

SECTION 12

2-6-0 Class 2 78000
Mixed-Traffic Locomotives
Introduced: 1952
Total: 65

The BR standard Class 2 2-6-0 was simply the LMS Ivatt design of 1946, modified in detail to bring it into line with the new standard types. The Ivatt engines had proved to be reliable and economical, as well as being first-class performers for their size. The low axle-load gave them a wide route availability throughout the BR system, and, it will be recalled, further examples of the LMS design had been constructed for use on other Regions in the early days of nationalisation.

The BR version had slightly cleaner lines than the original, with a short drop-plate ahead of the cylinders, to the footplate at buffer beam level,and with smoother contour to the cab sides and matching tender cab. The LMS top feed was replaced by the BR clack valve arrangement, and a sturdy-looking standard chimney set the seal on their new identity — but the parentage remained obvious. The boiler remained the same, with a tube heating surface of 924sq ft and a firebox heating surface of 101sq ft, giving a total evaporative heating surface of 1025sq ft. The superheater heating surface was 124sq ft. The grate area was 17.5sq ft. Boiler pressure was 200lb psi, and tractive effort at 85 per cent boiler pressure was 18 513lb, compared to 17 400lb for the LMS version, which had cylinders of 16in diameter by 24in stroke, whereas the BR version had the diameter increased to 16½in. Engine weight in full working order, for the BR engines, was 49tons 5cwt, compared to 47tons 2cwt (for LMS Nos 6400-6464) and 48tons 9cwt (for LMS Nos 6465-6527.) The tender, however, weighed slightly less, at 36tons 17cwt full, compared to 37tons 3cwt; the capacity remained the same.

The engines were built as follows:

Nos 78000-78009	Darlington	1952/3
Nos 78010-78019	Darlington	1953/4
Nos 78020-78044	Darlington	1954
Nos 78045-78054	Darlington	1954
Nos 78055-78064	Darlington	1956

When new, Nos 78000-78009, were allocated to the Western Region; Nos 78010-78019 were for the Eastern and North Eastern; Nos 78020-78044 were for the London Midland; Nos 78045-78054 were for the Scottish Region; and Nos 78055-78064 were for the London Midland. In each case the operating Region was also responsible for maintenance.

First of class withdrawn: 78015 (1963)
Last of class withdrawn: 78062 (1967)
Examples preserved: 78019, 78022*

* No 78022 was still in Barry Scrapyard at the time of writing.

Below: Standard Class 2 2-6-0 engine. The tender was type BR3, and the boiler was classified type BR8. Parent office for the design was Derby.

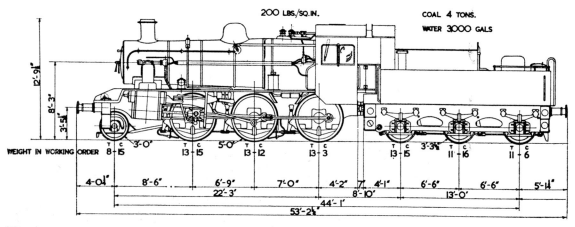

Top left: Ivatt LMS parentage was obvious in the case of the BR standard Class 2 2-6-0s (and the equivalent 2-6-2T) and only detail alterations distinguish the 78000 series. Most noticeable was the smoother appearance of the cab, the repositioned boiler feed clack valves and the small fallplate ahead of the cylinders. No 78019 was photographed at Kirkby Stephen shed; Whitsun weekend 1958./*R. M. Lush*

Centre left: The tender design for the BR Class 2 lightweight Moguls closely followed the Ivatt pattern, but had a modified contour to the forward cab portion, and roller bearing axleboxes were fitted. No. 78038 was in strange territory on 5 July 1964, working the LCGB 'Surrey Wanderer' railtour between Tulse Hill and Beckenham Junction on the Southern Region; it is seen leaving Crystal Palace Tunnel. The engine has BR AWS fitted, with some of the equipment visible on the running plate ahead of the cab./*Brian Stephenson*

Below: First of the class, No 78000 pictured here at Andover whilst running-in after repair at Swindon Works, where it had received un-lined BR Brunswick green livery in place of the original lined black. GWR style lampbrackets and ATC have been fitted. The engine had been out of traffic for the previous 10 months. The BR standard version of these Moguls had the normal slide type of regulator valve, in the dome, but the rodding to the handle in the cab was external./*G. Wheeler*

SECTION 13

2-6-2T Class 3 82000
Mixed-Traffic Locomotives
Introduced: 1952
Total: 45

The Standard Class 3 2-6-2T, and the corresponding 2-6-0 (see page 94) were introduced because of the existence of a number of routes having a 16-ton axle load restriction, which the Class 4 2-6-0 and 2-6-4T designs could not meet, whilst a more powerful engine than the Class 2 category was desirable.

There was no existing LMS boiler to suit engines in the Class 3 category, because the Ivatt Mogul boiler for the Class 4 was too heavy (although dimensionally suitable) and it was therefore decided to adapt the Swindon No 4 boiler. This allowed existing flanging blocks to be made use of, but the barrel was shortened by $5\frac{13}{16}$in, and a dome was added to what had been a domeless boiler when constructed for the GWR 2-6-2Ts of the 5100 and 8100 classes, and the 5600 0-6-2Ts. In other respects, including constructional detail, the boiler and fittings were brought into line with the new standard specifications, with an 18-element superheater in place of the Swindon 7-element design.

The principal dimensions were as follows: two cylinders 17½in diameter by 26in stroke; coupled wheels of 5ft 3in diameter; boiler pressure 200lb psi; tube heating surfaces 923 54sq ft; firebox heating surface 118 42sq ft; superheater 184 50sq ft; grate area 20.35sq ft; tractive effort at 85 per cent boiler pressure was 21 490lb.

The engines were built as follows:

Nos 82000-82009	Swindon	1952
Nos 82010-82019	Swindon	1952
Nos 82020-82029	Swindon	1954
Nos 82030-82034	Swindon	1954/5
Nos 82035-82044	Swindon	1955

Below: Standard Class 3 2-6-2T. The boiler was type BR6. Parent office for the design was Swindon. Total weight in full working order was 74tons 1cwt.

Right: No 82014 in as-built condition, at Eastleigh shed on 30 August 1952. The domed version of the Swindon boiler was classified BR6./*Pursey C. Short*

Below right: Standard Class 3 2-6-2T No 82003, at work on a West Midlands area suburban train. Such duties were subsequently handled by diesel multiple-unit railcars, and orders for further engines were cancelled with the completion of No 82044 at Swindon in 1955./*R. J. Blenkinsop*

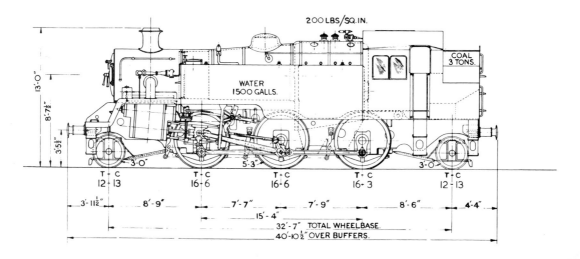

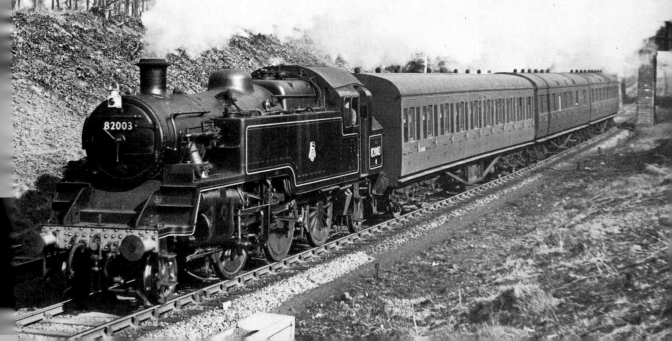

Top left: No 82034 skirts the sands at Goodrington with a Manchester-Torquay-Kingswear train on 17 June 1955. This attractive stretch of line now forms part of the route of the Torbay Steam Railway./*P. B. Whitehouse*

Left: Swindon painted some of the Class 3 2-6-2Ts in BR green livery when they returned for general repair. Some were in unlined green, such as No 82007 seen here, with large BR totem; later, some were fully lined out. A small grab rail had been added to the boiler top, ahead of the dome, by the time this picture was taken, at Swindon. The engine is flanked by two former Taff Vale 0-6-2Ts, Nos 347/78./*M. J. Norman*

Above: Class M7 0-4-4T No 30104 and standard Class 3 2-6-2T No 82016 double-head the 12.41pm Saturdays-only Fawley-Eastleigh train out of Redbridge, on 5 December 1959. The pair make a fascinating comparison of two phases of tank engine design!/*J. C. Haydon*

The BR building programme for 1954 included Nos 82045-82054, for the Western Region, and Nos 82055-82062 for the North Eastern Region. These were to have been built at Swindon, but the order was cancelled.

The engines were allocated to the following Regions for operational use, when new:

(The Region responsible for maintenance was the Western, for the entire class) Western Region: Nos 82000-82009; 82030-82044. Southern Region: Nos 82010-82029.

Civil engineering progress overtook the Class 3 engines and latterly the larger Class 4s could be used over many of the routes for which the smaller engines had been conceived, whilst in due course the diesel railcar fleet took over many of the workings formerly handled by the 2-6-2Ts.

First of class withdrawn: 82002/8/43 (1964)
Last of class withdrawn: 82029 (1967)
None preserved

SECTION 14

2-6-2T Class 2 84000
Mixed-Traffic Locomotives
Introduced: 1953
Total: 30

Ivatt's 2-6-2T passenger tank engine version of his 1946 Class 2 Mogul, for the LMS, was logically adopted for inclusion in the BR standard range along with the 2-6-0. Since nationalisation further engines had been built, including some for the Southern Region, and just as in the case of the corresponding 2-6-0, the class had proved to be efficient performers and easy to maintain, whilst having wide route availability.

The design was altered only so far as to include the new BR standard fittings, such as boiler feed clack valves in place of LMS-type top feed, and external regulator rodding. The boiler design was the same, with a tube heating surface of 924sq ft and a firebox heating surface of 101sq ft, giving a total evaporative heating surface of 1025sq ft. The superheater heating surface was 124sq ft. The grate area was 17.5sq ft. As in the case of the 78000 class the two cylinders were of 16½in diameter by 24in stroke. Boiler pressure was 200lb psi and tractive effort at 85 per cent boiler pressure was 18 513lb. Weight in full working order was 66 tons 5 cwt, compared to 63 tons 5cwt for the original LMS series.

The engines were built as follows:

Nos 84000-84019	Crewe	1953
Nos 84020-84029	Darlington	1957

The Darlington batch was originally scheduled for the 1953 building programme. Nos 84000-84019 were originally allocated to the London Midland Region, which also maintained them, and Nos 84020-84029 were for operation on the Southern Region, but allocated to the LM for maintenance.

The spread of dieselisation, with railcars of various types, overtook the class at an early stage and no further orders were contemplated.

First of class withdrawn: 84012 (1963)
Last of class withdrawn: 84028 (1965)
None preserved

Below: Standard Class 2 2-6-2T. The boiler was classified type BR8. Parent office for the design was Derby.

200 LBS/SQ.IN.

WATER 1350 GALLS.
COAL 3 TONS.

WEIGHT IN WORKING ORDER

12'-9½' 8'-3' 3'-5½'

12-10 13-12 14-0 13-13 12-10

4'-0¼' 8'-6' 6'-9' 7'-0' 8'-0" 4'-6¼'
30'-3"
38'-9½'

Above: Only 30 locomotives were constructed to the BR standard Class 2 2-6-2T design, and the final locomotive of the Darlington batch is seen here. The engines were at first fitted with vacuum control gear for motor-train working, but the gear had been removed from No 84029 by the time this picture was taken, at Eastleigh, on 22 April 1961. The overall appearance of the class closely followed Ivatt's LMS design except for the fallplate ahead of the cylinders, the BR standard chimney, boiler feed clack valves, and slightly modified cab at gutter level./*C. P. Boocock*

Centre left: Working bunker-first with a local to Maidstone, No 84020 is seen leaving Ashford in May 1958, and the array of footsteps and grab rails is well illustrated. These replaced the metal ladder of the original Ivatt design, as seen in the illustration of No 1206 on page 41./*P. Ransome-Wallis*

Bottom left: The vacuum control gear for push-pull working is clearly visible on the front of No 84025, seen double-heading BR standard Class 4 2-6-4T No 80038 on an Ashford-Maidstone train, passing the site of the old LCDR station at Ashford. The widespread introduction of diesel railcars displaced these engines from auto-train workings, and similar duties./*Derek Cross*

89

SECTION 15

4-6-2 Class 8P 71000
Express Passenger Locomotive
Introduced: 1954
Total: 1
'Duke of Gloucester'

When the range of new standard engines was in the planning stage, provision was made for a large express passenger Pacific design to be included, although there was no immediate need for further engines of the type on BR. This Pacific was envisaged as a modified Stanier 'Duchess' 4-6-2, with four cylinders and double blastpipe and chimney and bar frames.

In October 1952 the terrible accident at Harrow & Wealdstone station wrecked the LMR Pacific No 46202 *Princess Anne*, which had only recently entered traffic after conversion from Stanier's experimental 'Turbomotive'. This tragedy left a gap in the number of 8P Pacifics available to the London Midland Region, and Riddles took this opportunity to introduce the new Class 8P standard design, in prototype form, in order to gain running experience until such a time as orders could be placed for quantity construction. Thus was born No 71000 *Duke of Gloucester*, completed at Crewe in 1954. It was the subject of special financial authorisation and was not included in any regular building programme.

The engine, as actually constructed, represented quite a departure from the outline scheme of a modified Stanier Pacific, and also from the range of new standard two-cylinder types, including the smaller Class 6 and 7 Pacifics, which had Walschaerts valve gear and piston valves. Riddles settled for a three-cylinder engine, and the problems of the inside valve gear were overcome by driving the inside cylinder on to the leading axle, and by applying rotary cam poppet valve gear. The 'Britannia' boiler barrel and firebox flanging blocks were retained, but there was an enlarged grate area. A double chimney and blast pipe was fitted, but in all other important respects the design followed 'Britannia' practice, with 6ft 2in diameter coupled wheels and roller bearings on all axles.

The principal dimensions of No 71000 were as follows: three cylinders 18in diameter by 28in stroke; coupled wheels 6ft 2in diameter; boiler pressure 250lb psi; tube heating surfaces 2264sq ft; firebox heating surface 226sq ft; superheater heating surface 677sq ft; grate area 48.6sq ft. Tractive effort at 85 per cent boiler pressure was 39 080lb.

The tender fitted was unique to this engine, and was classified type BR1J. This had a capacity of 10tons of coal and 4325gal of water, and weighed 53tons 14cwt in full working order. A steam-operated coal pusher was fitted. This tender was originally intended for Class 9F 2-10-0 No 92150 and was modified for use with No 71000. The tender of

Below: BR standard Class 8 4-6-2 three-cylinder express passenger engine, with British-Caprotti valve gear. The boiler was type BR13 and the tender was type BR1J with steam-operated coal pusher. Parent office for the design was Derby. Total weight of engine and tender in full working order was 154tons 19cwt.

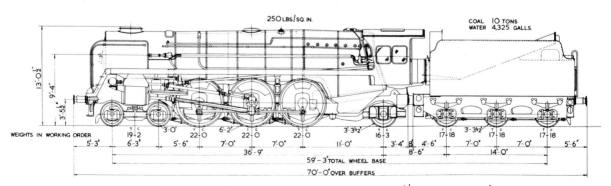

Top: No 71000 *Duke of Gloucester,* the final essay in British express passenger steam locomotive design, completed at Crewe works in 1954, and destined for a relatively short and solitary career, with the modernisation plan bringing about the change to diesel and electric traction soon afterwards, and no further orders placed for steam. Fitted with British-Caprotti valve gear, it was basically an enlarged 'Britannia', but with three cylinders, a larger grate area (all other boiler dimensions remaining the same;) and double blastpipe and chimney./*British Rail*

Above: No 71000 *Duke of Gloucester* fitted with front end indicator shelter and undergoing controlled road tests on the Western Region, arriving at Westbury with dynamometer car and 18 coaches. The engine portion and cylinders were really excellent, but the boiler performance and efficiency were not satisfactory at the higher power outputs. Vibration at the rear caused the firebed to be displaced and broken up, due to the undamped coil springs of the trailing truck. On the credit side, this engine was the most economical in steam consumption per indicated horsepower of any on record, in Britain or abroad, so far as single expansion is concerned. It only used 9per cent more steam per horsepower than the best Chapelon Compound, with all the latter's complication. If time had allowed, the design could have been investigated fully, and there is no doubt that the later engines of the type would have been truly superb examples of the express passenger power class élite — had they ever been built./*G. Wheeler*

type BRIE originally allotted to No 71000 then went to the 2-10-0 in exchange.

The Class 8P Pacific was stationed at Crewe North Shed and worked over the West Coast main line, often on the 'Midday Scot'. Although a very capable and powerful engine it gained a reputation for being heavy on coal, and it was acknowledged that further study would be needed before the design went into quantity production. The engine was an adequate steam producer but it placed heavy demands upon the fireman at the higher power outputs, and the LMR crews preferred their Stanier 'Duchess' Pacifics to the newcomer.

Events overtook the engine, and the decision to cease steam locomotive construction, and to change to diesel and electric traction, was made when No 71000 was still a comparatively new engine. The necessary studies to get the correct boiler proportions and draughting at the front end were not justified, and the engine ran out its days unaltered. Depite the draughting problems, and when given a keen crew, it nevertheless achieved some really excellent performances.

A strange twist of fate overtook the engine after withdrawal from service in November 1962. The British Railways Board decided to retain the Caprotti cylinders and gear as a static museum exhibit, and this portion of the engine was removed before selling the rest to Woodham Brothers of Barry, for scrap. In 1974 a move was made to rescue the engine for preservation, and it is now at Loughborough, on the former GCR line, awaiting full restoration, with cylinders reinstated by the Main Line Steam Trust.

Engine withdrawn: 1962
Engine preserved: 1964

Left: Standing in the sunlight at Camden shed on 31 May 1962 No 71000 *Duke of Gloucester,* showing the BR AWS fitting below the buffer beam, with protective shield behind the coupling. The smoke deflector handrails were retained on this engine, unlike the 'Britannias'./*M. Pope*

Below: Evidently recently out of Crewe after overhaul and repainting, No 71000 *Duke of Gloucester,* seen near Stafford with a West Coast express, in clean lined green livery. The trailing truck had coil springing, as opposed to the laminated springs of the Class 6 and 7 Pacifics, which had been criticised for hard-riding. The solitary 8P engine suffered from the same fate which had befallen so many prototypes in the saga of steam, by being a one-off job, which meant she was not fully appreciated by the men who worked her and who were more accustomed to the Stanier Pacifics. Given time to learn the engine's characteristics and given quantity construction, the men would have proved her true worth./*J. B. Bucknall*

SECTION 16

2-6-0 Class 3 77000
Mixed-Traffic Locomotives
Introduced: 1954
Total: 20

Between their conception and construction, the standard Class 3 Moguls were made to some degree unnecessary, because civil engineering progress had improved many of the lines for which they were designed, with the result that the larger Class 4 engines were permitted. Only 20 engines of the type were constructed, and further orders waived, but in any case the changeover to diesel railcars for branch-line services soon reduced the usefulness of such engines.

The design was the tender engine twin of the Class 3 2-6-2Ts in the 82000 series, and featured the same Swindon boiler, adapted to BR specification; the principal dimensions were the same and are shown on page 84. The tender attached was type BR2A, with a capacity of 6tons of coal and 3500gal of water. The engine weighed 57tons 0cwt in full working order, and the tender weighed 42tons 3cwt, giving a total weight of 99tons 13cwt in full working order.

The engines were built as follows:

Nos 77000-77019   Swindon   1954

When new, the engines were allocated to the North Eastern (Nos 77000-77004; 77010-77014) and Scottish Regions (Nos 77005-77009; 77015-77019), with the Eastern/North Eastern responsible for maintenance in both cases.

First of class withdrawn: 77010 (1965)
Last of class withdrawn: 77014 (1967)
None preserved

Below: Standard BR Class 3 2-6-0. The boiler was type BR6 and was based upon the Swindon No 4, with dome added. Parent office for the design was Swindon. Tender was type BR2A.

Right: Type BR2A tender, attached to Class 3 2-6-0 No 77009, with a capacity of 3500gal of water and 6tons of coal, showing the layout of ladder and grab rails, with large footblocks on rear of tank top./*British Rail WR*

Below right: Second engine of the batch of 20 built at Swindon in 1954, No 77001 of the standard Class 3 design, intended for routes with a 16ton axle load restriction. The cab was of later BR standard type, with fall plate re-introduced, hinged from the front of the tender to rest on the rearward extension of the cab floor. Gangway doors were fitted between engine and tender, and there were no draught screens./*Ian Allan Library*

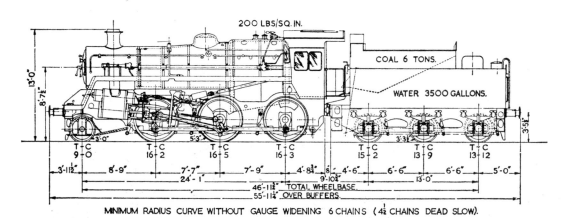

MINIMUM RADIUS CURVE WITHOUT GAUGE WIDENING 6 CHAINS (4½ CHAINS DEAD SLOW).

Top left: Standard Class 3 2-6-0 No 77012 and ex NER 0-6-0 No 65090, double-heading the 11.20am Blackpool Central-Newcastle train; seen leaving Tebay on 11 September 1954. The Mogul has a cable from the cab to the front coupling, to allow the engine to be released from the rear of a train, when on banking duty./*J. E. Wilkinson*

Bottom left: A distinctive feature of the Class 3 Moguls was their tall and shapely chimney, and the effect of the wider Class 4 chimney, seen here on No 77005, is quite surprising. The engine was photographed on colliery shunting work, near Motherwell. Detail changes, apart from the chimney substitution, include lowered lampbracket on the smokebox door and steel guard behind the screw coupling, to protect the BR AWS installation./*A. Swain*

Below: Another view of No 77012, taken some four years later, by which time it had received the later version of the BR totem on the tender. The engine was photographed at Whitby Town on 1 August 1958, backing down to couple-up to the 3.14pm train to Malton. Alongside is one of the new Metro-Cammell diesel multiple-unit sets, destined to oust steam from the type of passenger duties for which the Class 3 2-6-0s were designed./*M. Mensing*

SECTION 17

2-10-0 Class 9F 92000
Heavy Goods Locomotives
Introduced: 1954
Total: 251

The last of the dozen BR standard steam locomotive designs to appear was probably the most successful, yet destined to be very short-lived by steam's yardstick. In the original proposals for standard engines the role of heavy freight engine was to be fulfilled by a 2-8-2, with boiler, cylinders and many other details in common with the 'Britannias'. The driving wheel diameter was to be 5ft 3in, to improve upon the running speeds of existing 2-8-0 types. This proposed Class 8 Mikado would have been a useful mixed-traffic engine, but from the freight train performance viewpoint the increase in adhesion over existing 2-8-0s was small, in relation to the increase in potential power.

The heavy freight engine was low on the building priority list, as the post-war influx of ex-WD 'Austerities' and Stanier 2-8-0s had eased the demands for freight power. When design work did commence, early in 1951, the 2-8-2 concept was seriously questioned and Riddles — no doubt with his wartime experience with the WD 2-10-0 in mind — opted in favour of a 2-10-0 wheel arrangement, with 5ft 0in diameter coupled wheels and a wide firebox. This meant that the boiler could not be standard with that on the 'Britannias', but all other components were to be standardised to a high degree; in fact,

however, the finalised design had no major constituent parts common to standard Pacifics or 4-6-0s, and comparatively few smaller parts, except the tenders and cab fittings.

The diameter of the boiler barrel was the same, at the front, as that of the 'Britannias' and the same flanging blocks were used for the smokebox tubeplate, but the taper of the barrel upwards was by only 4in to 73in, compared to 77½in for the Pacific boiler; the reduced diameter at the back end was because the boiler had to be pitched high, in

Below: Standard Class 9F 2-10-0, in the as-built condition of the first batch constructed at Crewe, with type BR1G tender. The boiler was type BR9. The main centre pair of driving wheels were flangeless. Parent office for the design was Brighton. Total weight in full working order, with type BR1G tender attached was 139tons 4cwt.

Right: Standard Class 9F 2-10-0 No 92009, of the first Crewe-built batch of 15 engines, seen in brand new condition, attached to a type BR1G tender, with inset bunker and a capacity of 5000gal and 7tons of coal; photographed on the Midland main line. The frames for the 9F design were particularly rigid and robust. Plain bearing axleboxes were used throughout the engine, but the tenders had roller bearing axleboxes./*Ian Allan Library*

Below right: The large type BR1F tender with a capacity of 5625gal and 7tons of coal, seen attached to Class 9F 2-10-0 No 92010, photographed at Holbeck shed on 11 May 1961. All five tender variations were of the later type with fallplate re-introduced to suit the cab design, which was of the improved type, introduced to reduce draughts. By the time this picture was taken No 92010 had the enlarged footstep added below the smokebox door, and sandbox fillers raised above running plate./*G. W. Morrison*

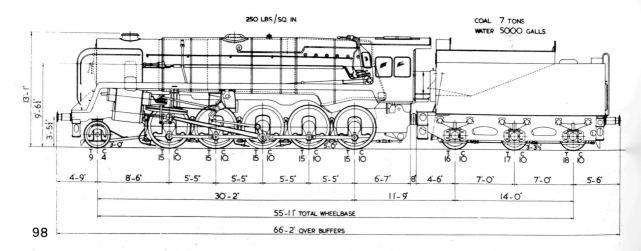

Above: Crosti-boiler Class 9F 2-10-0 No 92022, photographed at Wellingborough in August 1955. What appeared to be a normal chimney at the front was in fact only used for lighting-up purposes and then closed. The hot gases, on leaving the boiler tube bank, were turned back on themselves, in the smokebox and passed through a further series of tubes in the secondary drum, which acted as a pre-heater for the feed water, before being exhausted via the multiple blastpipes and long thin chimney on the boiler side. The secondary drum was beneath the main boiler barrel, between the frames and had a final secondary smokebox, with the door visible below the main smokebox. Note the location of sandbox fillers for the leading coupled wheels, high up on the sloping front to the running plate./*A. W. Flowers*

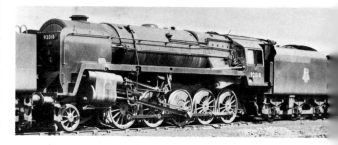

Above right: The type BR1C tender, attached to 9F 2-10-0 No 92018, with a capacity of 4725gal and 9tons of coal; photographed at Cricklewood on 20 July 1958. All the tenders ran on six wheels of 3ft 3½in diameter; only the weight in working order varied, the wheelbase and overall length of engine and tender remaining constant. Steam brakes were provided on both engine and tender and could be operated either directly by means of a gradual steam brake valve, or in conjunction with the vacuum brake. The coupled and tender wheels were braked by means of a single block on each wheel. Two ashpan raking doors were later introduced at front and back of the firebox, above the rear coupled wheels./*R. K. Evans*

Centre left: Cab-end view of Crosti-boilered Class 9F 2-10-0 No 92028, showing the additional grab rail on the cab side and footplate below; photographed on shed at Toton on 25 March 1956. To accommodate the Crosti layout within the British L2 loading gauge, the main boiler had to be smaller than standard and was more sharply tapered, with the single large pre-heater below. The main boiler was pitched 9ft 11¾in above rail level, the highest pitch ever applied in Britain, and one leaving the minimum of space for boiler mountings./*J. Buckingham*

Bottom left: In an attempt to improve conditions in the cab and aid visibility, the Crosti engines received smoke deflector plates, alongside the exhaust on the boiler side, as seen on No 92023; photographed at Holbeck shed on 14 December 1958. Conditions were sometimes very unpleasant for the enginemen, due to smoke and steam entering the cab and swirling around the footplate; this was a direct result of the proximity of the exhaust and the need to contain it within the loading gauge, on the right hand side of the main boiler barrel./*C. Sheard*

Above: Without doubt, one of the hardest duties worked by the 9Fs was the Tyne Dock-Consett iron ore trains, normally composed of nine bogie hopper wagons, plus brakevan, and weighing some 787tons, over gradients as steep as 1 in 35. The 10 engines of the class used for these trains were fitted with two air pumps midway along the running plate, for operating the doors on the hopper wagons. They were allocated to Tyne Dock shed, where No 92097 was photographed on 14 September 1963./*V. C. K. Allen*

order that the grate should clear the rear coupled wheels, whilst remaining within the L2 loading gauge. The grate was flat over the rear half and sloped at the front. A different design of regulator, in the form of a sliding grid throttle in the dome, was fitted and outside rodding was retained. When new this throttle design was very troublesome and the design was modified after some 16 engines had been built, to prevent excessive slipping at slow speed with heavy loads, when the throttle was found to be difficult to close.

The principal dimensions of the engines were as follows: two cylinders 20in diameter by 28in stroke; coupled wheels 5ft 0in diameter; boiler pressure 250lb psi; tube heating surfaces 1835sq ft; firebox heating surface 179sq ft, giving a total evaporative heating surface of 2014sq ft; superheating surface 535sq ft; grate area 40.2sq ft. Tractive effort at 85 per cent boiler pressure was 39 667lb. These dimensions apply to the first batch constructed and also apply to all subsequent batches, except the Franco-Crosti engines.

The decision was taken to incorporate the latest form of Crosti boiler and heating equipment in Nos 92020-92029, after these engines had been authorised for construction as engines of the normal standard type. Their construction was delayed whilst the necessary design alterations were finalised. It was thought that the Crosti experiment might achieve worthwhile coal economies, at a time when the supply and cost of coal was critical in Britain. The principal dimensions for these

Above: A Tyne Dock-Consett iron ore train in full cry on the 1 in 35 gradient between Stanley and Annfield Plain, on 14 August 1962. The leading 2-10-0 is No 92064, fitted with the special air pumps for working the hopper doors. The banking engine is No 92167, fitted with Berkley mechanical stoker (one of three so fitted, Nos 92165-92167) and busy dusting the countryside with particles of ash and fines !/*J. M. Rayner*

Above right: One locomotive, No 92079, was selected for the special role of main banking engine on the Lickey incline, in 1956-58, and was fitted with the large electric headlight previously carried by the ex-Midland Railway 0-10-0 banking engine No 58100. Other engines of the 9F class were used from time to time, including Nos 92005 and 92231. Seen at the rear of a Bristol-Bradford train, at Bromsgrove, No 92079 was photographed on 10 June 1956. One hopes the cattle wagon ahead of the engine was unoccupied, otherwise the occupants were about to be treated to a deafening explosion of sound as the 2-10-0 barked its way up the 1 in 37 incline !/*A. W. Martin*

Centre right: No 92178 was delivered new with a double blastpipe and chimney, and ran trials without the smoke deflector plates fitted. The engine is seen whilst on controlled road tests on the Western Region with dynamometer car attached, in January 1958. Loads of up to 650 tons were handled and the engine demonstrated an increment in power output and saving in coal consumption./*E. S. Cox*

Bottom right: Following the double blastpipe and chimney application to No 92178, new construction of Class 9Fs had this modification, from No 92183 to 92250. Four existing engines were also fitted, Nos 92000/1/6, 92079. The chimney was well proportioned and made quite a handsome addition to the 2-10-0's appearance as seen here on No 92187, which has the large type BR1F tender attached/*David J. Dippie*

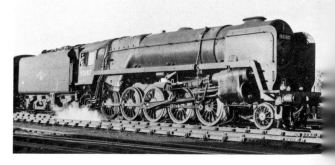

engines were as follows (where different from standard): tube heating surfaces 1297sq ft; firebox heating surface 158sq ft, giving a total evaporative heating surface of 1455sq ft. To this total was added a preheater of 1021sq ft and exhaust steam jacket 57sq ft. The superheater surface was 411sq ft. Maximum axle load was 15.95tons for the engine, compared to 15.5tons standard, and weight in working order was 90.2 tons compared to 86.7tons.

The reduction in coal consumption did not match the predictions of the Crosti people, and the maintenance costs of the tubular feed water heaters were high; with severe corrosion problems with the chimney and final smokebox. By 1958 the Crosti engines were mostly laid aside, and the following year a start was made upon abandoning the scheme, when No 92026, had its heater equipment removed and normal draughting applied. In this converted form (which incidentally took some two years to complete) the 10 engines retained their original smaller boiler and firebox with the smaller evaporative capacity, and they were used on duties which did not demand high boiler output. In this converted form the ex-Crosti engines had the following non-standard dimensions: tube heating surfaces 1274sq ft; firebox heating surface 158sq ft giving a total evaporative heating surface of 1432sq ft. The superheater gave 411sq ft. Maximum axle load was down to 15.3tons and the engine weight in full working order was reduced to 83.6tons, compared to 90.2tons as Crosti-fitted, or the 86.7tons of the normal 9Fs.

Two other experiments were tried upon the 2-10-0s, to investigate the value of

Above: Class 9F 2-10-0 No 92024 after removal of the Crosti fittings, and restored to normal draughting, but retaining the reduced proportions of boiler and firebox, and odd-shaped smokebox. No smoke deflectors were fitted to the converted engines. In this modified form the former Crosti engines were somewhat less powerful than the standard 9Fs because of the smaller boiler and firebox carried. The high pitch of the boiler was retained and the chimney must rank as one of the smallest ever produced for use on a British main line locomotive. */J. B. Bucknall*

mechanical stoking and the value of the Giesl exhaust system. The mechanical stoker was the American Berkley design and was applied to Nos 92165-92167, built at Crewe in 1958. The aim was to increase the firing rate beyond the capacity of a fireman thereby increasing the evaporation to a degree where the engines could work fully-fitted freights at improved schedules, with loads of 50 or more laden 16-ton wagons. Existing Class C schedules had a maximum speed of 42 mph and a 9F 2-10-0 could handle 35-37 wagons of 16 tons capacity, but the demands made upon the fireman were very high on some sections of line. The experiment showed that coal consumption was increased, but that a gain of about 10 per cent evaporation (after modifications to the grate) was possible; specially crushed coal had to be provided. The equipment was removed from the engines in 1962 and one of them, No 92167, survived in hand-fired form as the last of the 9F class in service (except for preserved engines), oddly running its last few duties as a makeshift 2-8-2, with the rear side rods removed, in June 1968.

Top right: Another view of No 92024, a former Crosti engine, photographed at Crewe works after repair and finished in black livery without BR emblem on the tender. Large central footstep added to front end below the smokebox door, and top lamp-bracket lowered to side of numberplate./*J. R. Carter*

Centre right: A Fawley-Birmingham special oil train on the Lickey incline, with Class 9F 2-10-0 No 92248, fitted with double chimney, at the head, plus a pair of banking engines at the rear; photographed on 23 April 1964. A striking reminder of the struggle for adhesion which steam power constantly experienced on Lickey, and which provided the onlooker with an impressive cacophony of sound./*Derek Cross*

Below: Another double-chimney 9F, No 92210, on passenger duty over the Somerset & Dorset. The engine was photographed near Shepton Montague on 21 July 1962 at the head of the 7.40am Saturdays-only Bradford-Bournemouth train. The 9Fs were ideal engines for this difficult route, but they arrived at the eleventh hour. No steam heating provision was made on the 9Fs, thus restricting them to passenger work during the summer timetable./*Ivo Peters*

The Giesl oblong ejector was fitted to No 92250 in 1959, when the existing double chimney was removed and the characteristic flat Giesl chimney applied. The objective was to increase power for a given coal consumption, or to economise in fuel at any level of power output, whilst using poor grade fuel. Results were disappointing when the engine was subjected to tests, and no further applications of the ejector were authorised for the class, although No 92250 ran with the system for the rest of its life.

The engines were built as follows:

Nos 92000-92014	Crewe	1954
Nos 92015-92019	Crewe	1954
Nos 92020-92029	Crewe	1955
Nos 92030-92049	Crewe	1954/5
Nos 92050-92086	Crewe	1955/6
Nos 92087-92096	Swindon	1956/7
Nos 92097-92134	Crewe	1956/7
Nos 92135-92177	Crewe	1957/8
Nos 92178-92202	Swindon	1957/8
Nos 92203-92220	Swindon	1959/60
Nos 92221-92250	Crewe	1958

The engines Nos 92178, 92183-92250 were built with double blastpipes and chimneys. Nos 92000/1/6 and 92079 were altered from single to double later. Five different tender types were attached to the class, as follows:

Type BRIB, Nos 92020-92029, 92060-92066 and 92097-92099; Type BRIC, Nos 92015-92019; 92045-92059, 92077-

92086, 92100-92139 and 92150-92164; Type BRIF, Nos 92010-92014, 92030-92044, 92067-92076, 92087-92096, 92140-92149 and 92168-92202; Type BRIG, Nos 92000-92009 and 92203-92250; Type BRIK (mechanical stoker), Nos 92165-92167.

The choice of tender depended largely upon the Regional allocation of each batch. When new these allocations were as follows: (the Region responsible for maintenance is shown in brackets.)

Western Region (WR): Nos 92000-92007; 92203-92250.
London Midland Region (LMR): Nos 92008-92009; 92015-92029; 92045-92059; 92077-92086; 92100-92139; 92150-92167.

Below: The Giesl oblong ejector was fitted to Class 9F 2-10-0 No 92250, after the engine had been in service for a year or so with a double chimney. The application was put to the test and the results were somewhat disappointing compared to the claims of the inventor, due in some degree to the already good draughting of the 2-10-0 design. No extension of the scheme was authorised, but No 92250 (which was the last steam locomotive built at Crewe) retained the Giesl ejector until withdrawal. The engine was photographed at Newport on 11 August 1963; a year and a half before withdrawal. */A. J. Wheeler*

Eastern Region (E/NE): Nos 92010-92014; 92030-92044; 92067-92076; 92087-92096; 92140-92149; 92168-92202.
North Eastern Region (E/NE): Nos 92060-92066; 92097-92099.

The Scottish Region never had a large allocation of these engines, apart from the borderline case of those working from Carlisle, although in retrospect the design would seem to have been ideal for some Scottish routes, including the Highland line passenger trains. Although intended for freight work, the 9F 2-10-0s gained a reputation as fast runners, and in the course of time they began to appear on summer express passenger duties. Quite a lot of publicity resulted from some very fast runs, with speeds around the 80-90mph mark, before officialdom clamped down firmly on such practice. The Somerset & Dorset line was excepted, and the class worked passenger trains over this difficult line in its final years before passenger working ceased. Their exploits on passenger trains were a fine tribute to their free running, despite the relatively small diameter of the driving wheels.

The modernisation plan spelled an early end to these fine machines and some had quite tragically short careers, being withdrawn whilst still in excellent condition. The Western Region withdrew its entire allocation during the course of 1965, including some engines built only five years earlier. The class was the last type of steam locomotive to be constructed for use on BR and two engines were of additional historic significance. No 92250 was the last steam engine built at Crewe, in December 1958, and No 92220 was the last steam engine built at Swindon, in

Above: The most famous freight engine of all time, and a representative of one of the finest British designs of the steam era — No 92220 *Evening Star*, the last new steam locomotive constructed at Swindon Works and the final new steam locomotive delivered to British Railways before the complete changeover to diesel and electric traction for new construction. Immediately selected for preservation, once its active service on BR was over, the engine was delivered to traffic in full passenger green livery and had a GWR-type copper cap to the double chimney. The nameplates fitted were of GWR Egyptian serif lettering style, and below each nameplate was a special commemorative plaque. No 92220 *Evening Star* is seen on strange territory at Clapham Junction. on 20 September 1964, working the Southern Counties Touring Society "Farewell to Steam" rail tour from Victoria to Yeovil. The engine is now in York Railway Museum./*Mrs. M. Stephenson*

March 1960. No 92220 was also the final steam engine built for use on British Railways, and was immediately scheduled for eventual preservation, being named *Evening Star* at a special ceremony at Swindon. Painted in full BR passenger green livery and fitted with a GWR style copper cap to its double chimney, No 92220 had the sad distinction of being the shortest-lived member of the class in service on BR, although it has since seen some further service in its preserved state.

First of class withdrawn: Nos 92034, 92169/70/1/5/6 (1964).
Last of class withdrawn: Nos 92077, 92160/7 (1968).
Examples preserved: 92203†, 92212*, 92220.

* *Still in Barry Scrapyard at time of writing.*
† *Now named* Black Prince.

Appendix 1

The LMS Diesels

H. G. Ivatt was responsible for the design and introduction of the pioneer main line diesels on the LMS. The first locomotive, No 10000, appeared in December 1947, just three weeks before the LMS lost its identity and became part of the new national system. The 1600hp design was intended to be comparable with a Class 4 steam engine, or when coupled to a second engine of the same type, to a Stanier Pacific. The 827 hp design was comparable to the class 2 2-6-2T.

Below: Heralds of a new era; twin diesels Nos 10000/1 working in multiple-unit on 1 June 1949 at the head of the first diesel-hauled 'Royal Scot', with carriages in red and cream livery. No 10001 was completed after nationalisation and did not carry the initials LMS along the side. Photographed in pouring rain, as the train passed Carpenders Park. Gangway doors in the nose ends were opened and the two locomotives were connected by a flexible walkthrough, of very restricted dimensions./*Rev. B. Whitworth*

Below: The first main-line diesel-electric express locomotive to enter service on a British Railway. H. G. Ivatt's classic Co-Co No 10000, completed by the LMS at Derby in December 1947. The power equipment was supplied, as a joint venture, by the English Electric Company, and the mechanical parts were designed and built by the LMS. The engine was a 16-cylinder Vee-type four cycle diesel, having a twelve hour rating of 1600hp at 750 rpm. No 10000 was photographed when new, leaving Luton with a Manchester-St Pancras express. The livery was black, with aluminium trim./*W. S. Garth*

Top: No 10800 was a diesel-electric Bo-Bo, of 827hp designed for branch line and secondary duties, and built by the North British Locomotive Co, in 1950. The engine was a 16-cylinder Davey Paxman, and the electrical equipment was by BTH. No 10800 ran trials on the Southern Region in 1953 and is seen here leaving Oxted station in the April of that year./*British Rail SR*

Above: The experimental Fell diesel-mechanical locomotive, No 10100, seen passing Tebay on a test run. Four 500hp 12-cylinder Paxman engines drove into a central gearbox, connected mechanically with the road wheels through differentials and fluid couplings. Two additional 6cylinder AEC 150hp engines provided the power for main engine superchargers and all auxiliaries. Total weight 120tons; tractive effort 25000lb. The only engine in the world ever turned out with sixty cylinders!/*J. E. Wilkinson*

Appendix 2

Named Locomotives

Showing the named locomotives of the classes constructed under Ministry of Supply and BR auspices.

2-8-0 'Austerity' WD
(see page 18)
WD 78672 Sir Guy Williams*
WD 78675 Sapper
WD 77337 Sir Guy Williams †
WD 79250 Major General McMullen
WD 79312 (BR No 90732) Vulcan‡

2-10-0 'Austerity' WD
(see page 28)
WD 73651 Gordon††
WD 73755 Longmoor
WD 73797 Sapper/Kitchener
WD 73798 (BR No 90773) North British
WD 73799 (BR No 90774) North British

4-6-2 Class 7 Mixed-Traffic
'Britannias'
(see page 53)
70000 Britannia
70001 Lord Hurcomb
70002 Geoffrey Chaucer

* On the Detmold Military Railway
† On the Longmoor Military Railway
‡ The last Austerity 2-8-0 built in Britain

†† Originally allocated the name Mountbatten

70003 John Bunyan
70004 William Shakespeare
70005 John Milton
70006 Robert Burns
70007 Couer-de-Lion
70008 Black Prince
70009 Alfred the Great
70010 Owen Glendower**
70011 Hotspur
70012 John of Gaunt
70013 Oliver Cromwell
70014 Iron Duke
70015 Apollo
70016 Ariel
70017 Arrow
70018 Flying Dutchman
70019 Lightning
70020 Mercury
70021 Morning Star
70022 Tornado
70023 Venus
70024 Vulcan
70025 Western Star

** In 1966 new nameplates were fitted, with the Welsh version of the name: Owain Glyndwr

Below: 'Britannia' Pacific No 70004 *William Shakespeare* photographed at Dover, with 'Golden Arrow' headboard and embellishments. The engine retains the special exhibition finish it was given for display at the 1951 Festival of Britain on London's South Bank. The standard nameplates for the 'Britannias' and the 'Clans' were of simple Gill Sans style, similar to, but smaller than, the LNER style. When new, these nameplates had a red background, later changed to black. */P. Ransome-Wallis*

70026 Polar Star
70027 Rising Star
70028 Royal Star
70029 Shooting Star
70030 William Wordsworth
70031 Byron***
70032 Tennyson
70033 Charles Dickens
70034 Thomas Hardy
70035 Rudyard Kipling
70036 Boadicea
70037 Hereward The Wake
70038 Robin Hood
70039 Sir Christopher Wren
70040 Clive of India
70041 Sir John Moore
70042 Lord Roberts
70043 Lord Kitchener
70044 Earl Haig
70045 Lord Rowallan
70046 Anzac
70048 The Territorial Army 1908-58
70049 Solway Firth
70050 Firth of Clyde
70051 Firth of Forth
70052 Firth of Tay
70053 Moray Firth
70054 Dornoch Firth

4-6-2 Class 6 Mixed-Traffic
'Clans'
(see page 62)
72000 Clan Buchanan
72001 Clan Cameron

*** *Believed to have carried unofficial nameplates in 1966, as* Lord Byron

Above: Refined simplicity. A single letterform, Gill Sans, was adopted by BR for locomotive nameplates, named train headboards, smokebox numberplates, and other items on show to the public. This neat and eminently legible style is well seen on 'Britannia' Pacific No 70037 *Hereward The Wake* leaving Liverpool Street, in May 1956, with the down 'Day Continental'. The main exceptions to this style were the 20 Southern Region Class 5 4-6-0s with 'King Arthur'-type nameplates, and the final 2-10-0 No 92220 *Evening Star,* which had GWR-style lettering./*R. E. Vincent*

72002 Clan Campbell
72003 Clan Fraser
72004 Clan MacDonald
72005 Clan MacGregor
72006 Clan MacKenzie
72007 Clan MacIntosh
72008 Clan MacLeod
72009 Clan Stewart

A further 15 engines were authorised for the 1955 building programme, but subsequently cancelled. As a matter of interest their intended names are listed:

72010 Hengist
72011 Horsa
72012 Canute
72013 Wildfire
72014 Firebrand
72015 Clan Colquhoun
72016 Clan Graham
72017 Clan MacDougall
72018 Clan MacLean
72019 Clan Douglas
72020 Clan Gordon

72021 Clan Hamilton
72022 Clan Kennedy
72023 Clan Lindsay
72024 Clan Scott

4-6-0 Class 5 Mixed-Traffic
(see page 66)
The Southern Region allocated names to 20 engines running on their lines. These were the same names as previously carried by 'King Arthur' class 4-6-0s Nos 30736-30755, and were of similar style, but new nameplates were cast, without the small 'King Arthur' class tag.

73080 Merlin
73081 Excalibur
73082 Camelot
73083 Pendragon
73084 Tintagel
73085 Melisande
73086 The Green Knight
73087 Linette
73088 Joyous Gard
73089 Maid of Astolat
73110 The Red Knight
73111 King Uther
73112 Morgan Le Fay
73113 Lyonesse
73114 Etarre
73115 King Pellinore
73116 Iseult
73117 Vivien
73118 King Leodegrance
73119 Elaine

4-6-2 Class 8P Express Passenger
(see page 90)
71000 Duke of Gloucester

2-10-0 Class 9F Heavy Freight
(see page 98)
92220 Evening Star

Since withdrawal from BR stock, three standard locomotives have been named, as follows:
4-6-0 Class 4 No 75029 The Green Knight.
2-10-0 Class 9F No 92203 Black Prince.
(Both these engines are preserved by David Shepherd, at the East Somerset Railway Cranmore shed).

4-6-0 Class 5 No 73050 City of Peterborough (Preserved by Peterborough Railway Society Limited).

Top: Nameplate of standard Class 5 4-6-0 No 73083 *Pendragon;* one of the Southern Region allocation which took the names formerly carried by 'King Arthur' class 4-6-0s. New plates were cast, without the small class label below the name./*British Rail SR*

Above: Egyptian-style serif letterforms, similar to the standard GWR type, were used for the special nameplates attached to No 92220 *Evening Star.* Small commemorative plates were fitted below, marking the naming ceremony at Swindon, on 18 March 1960./*Museum of British Transport*

Bibliography

The following books, which were referred to in the course of compiling this pictorial history, are thoroughly recommended to the reader in search of further information about H. G. Ivatt and R. A. Riddles, and their locomotives.

Bond, Roland C. *A Lifetime with Locomotives* Goose & Son
Bulleid, H. A. V. *Master Builders of Steam* Ian Allan Ltd
Cox, E. S. *Locomotive Panorama* (2 vols) Ian Allan Ltd
Cox, E. S. *Chronicles of Steam* Ian Allan Ltd
Cox, E. S. *British Railways Standard Steam Locomotives* Ian Allan Ltd

Pollock, D. R. and White, D. E. *The 2-8-0 and 2-10-0, Locomotives of the War Department, 1939-1945* Railway Correspondence and Travel Society
Reed, B. (editor) *Loco Profiles Nos 12, 33* Profile Publications
Rogers, Colonel H. C. B. *The Last Steam Locomotive Engineer: R. A. Riddles, CBE* George Allen & Unwin
Rowledge, P. *Engines of the LMS, built 1923-51* Oxford Publishing Co
Weekes, G. (editor) *BR Standard Britannia Pacifics* D. Bradford Barton Ltd
Wildish, Guy N. *Engines of War* Ian Allan Ltd

Below: Railwaymen's tributes adorn the front of BR standard Class 5 4-6-0 No 73093, photographed standing at Basingstoke shed on Sunday 9 July 1967, prior to running to Salisbury for withdrawal./*K. P. Lawrence*